SECRET LAKES

OF SOUTHERN VANCOUVER ISLAND

ADAM UNGSTAD

Third printing June 2013 by Friesens Corporation.
Printed in Canada.

Published by UNGSTAD Information Architects
www.ungstad.com

Ungstad, Adam, 1979 –
Secret Lakes of Southern Vancouver Island: Exploring the recreation, nature and history of 25 lakes from the Saanich Peninsula to the Sooke Hills.

ISBN 978-0-9880853-0-5

Maps: Daniel Cammiade (www.freakmaps.com)
Editing: Eric Anderson (www.chromoschema.com)
Layout & Design: Ross Macaulay (www.rossangus.com)

Cover photograph of Kemp Lake by Adam Ungstad.

To purchase this book in quantities for corporate use please contact
info@secretlakes.ca.

This book was printed on FSC-certified, acid-free paper,
processed chlorine free and printed with vegetable-based inks.

for Gabriel

Secret Lakes of Southern Vancouver Island

1. Durrance
2. Pease
3. Killarney
4. Fork
5. Eagles
6. Prospect
7. Elk/Beaver
8. Swan
9. Thetis
10. McKenzie
11. Prior
12. Langford
13. Glen
14. Florence
15. Lookout
16. Blinkhorn
17. Matheson
18. Glinz
19. Crabapple
20. Sheilds
21. Grass
22. Peden
23. Kemp
24. Spectacle
25. Heal

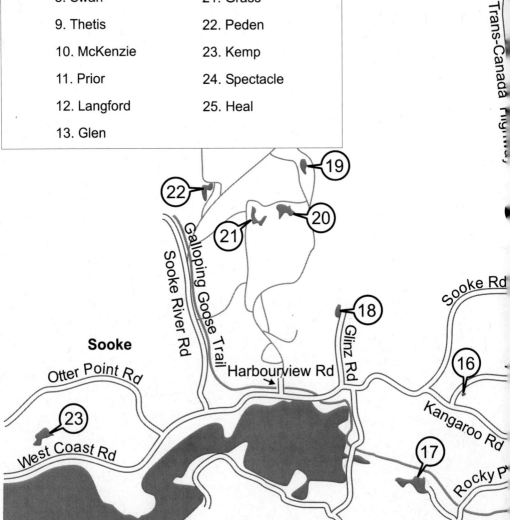

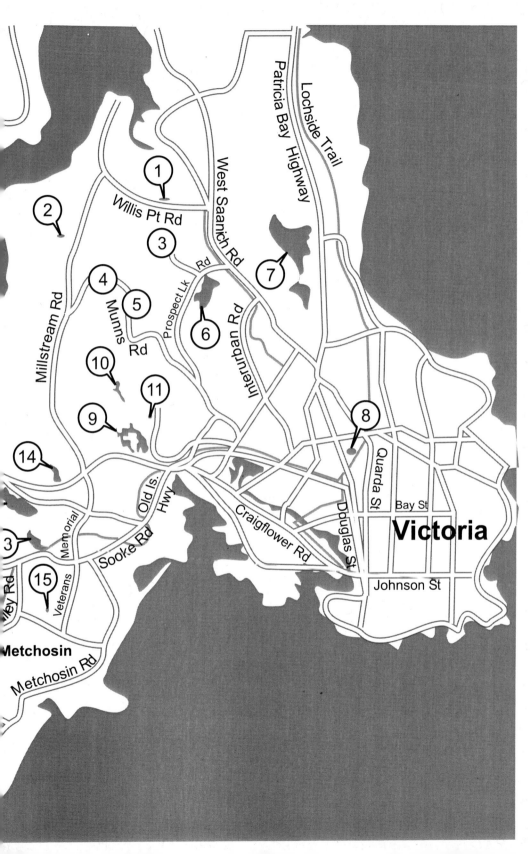

Contents

Acknowledgments

As with all great things, this book would not exist without the knowledge, talents, experience and support of many people.

In particular I'd like to thank my beautiful wife, Carly, for always supporting my grand ambitions and having the patience to let me chase after them.

For incredible diligence and high quality of work, huge gratitude and respect to Daniel Cammiade, Eric Anderson, and Ross Macaulay. For providing mentorship on the self-publishing process, thank you to Rebecca Kennel and Cynthia L'Hirondelle.

For contributing some downright amazing photographs, thank you to Adam Lee, Bill Irvine, Carly Macoun, City of Langford, Dennis Kangasniemi, District of Highlands, Eric Anderson, Mark Gustafson, Mike J. Munroe, The Prospect Lake Golf Course, Shane White, The Swan Lake Christmas Hill Nature Sanctuary, The Land Conservancy, and Tracy Clifford.

For contributing in other ways great and small, thank you to Allen Krutz, Caprina Valentine, Carol Ogborne, Dave Hill, Dennis Kangasniemi, Heather Skydt, Janet Mason, Jen Abrahamson, Jill Patterson, Jim Chapman, Kristi Calder, Laura Beckett, Lynn Wilson, Mary Haig-Brown, Michael Ross, Nancy Wise, Rick Nordin, Shawn Steele, Susan Lai, Tryce Blion, William & Danny, and Winona Pugh.

Thank you to my family, Dave, Edie, Leah and Jeremy, and my network of amazing friends who continually explore with me and always provide encouragement for my endeavours.

Last but not least, thank you for buying this book. I hope you put it to good use.

Killarney Lake in Mount Work Park. Photo by Adam Ungstad.

Introduction

This is the book I wanted to read seven years ago. When I first arrived in Victoria I didn't really know anyone, so I spent a lot of time on my bike. Being legally blind meant I couldn't drive, but I still had enough vision to explore by bicycle.

One sunny afternoon I "discovered" Thetis Lake on a ride, which left quite an impression on me. Each summer following I'd continue to explore the area by bike in search of new swimming holes. The building where I worked at the time backed on to the Galloping Goose Regional Trail, meaning that a refreshing after-work swim was only a 45 minute ride away. I could be in the lake by 5:15, with plenty of time left to enjoy the sun and the easy ride back home. I loved the experience of planning a new route, getting exercise on the way, and the refreshing swim once I arrived.

The idea for writing this book came to me late one night as I was scouring the internet for information about the remote lakes up in the Sooke Hills. Accessible only on foot or bike by wilderness trails, and with names like Crabapple and Grass I could barely contain my curiosity. What were these remote, undisturbed lakes like?

The information I could find was sketchy at best, and often contradictory. Sometimes people had different names for the same trail, and it was difficult to find any reliable maps. I wrote this book because I wanted to know everything in it – and I figured I might as well tell everyone else while I was at it.

I did have some moments of doubt along the way. I wondered if the extra attention for the lakes that the book would generate would be a good thing. "If you love it, leave it alone" I thought. Yet I couldn't let the idea go. I looked into it a bit more and found that keeping these ecosystems secret is not always what's best for them. I soon learned that the impact of recreation at a lake is considerably less than that of pollution, forestry, or development.

It goes without saying that these lakes must be preserved. In some cases lakes on private land are very well looked after, such as Maltby Lake. Yet land changes hands over time, and different owners have different objectives. For people to act to preserve something, they must first be aware of its value.

If we do not know, enjoy and respect our lakes we will not act to protect them. I wrote this book to educate and inspire people. The 25 lakes in this book are a small sampling of the estimated 18,000 lakes in the province of British Columbia – I hope that they will inspire you to enjoy and protect many more.

Adam Ungstad
May 2012

About this book

This book, first and foremost, is a guidebook. It is intended to take you to places you might not otherwise go, make the most of your time there, and to help you understand these lakes in their natural and historical contexts. As such, this book should be used as a guide-book rather than an authoritative source of scientific or historical information.

As the author I have made a tremendous effort to ensure the accuracy of the content this book, but as we all know, things change.

The water levels of a lake change based on the weather, while the boundaries of public and private land continually redraw themselves and new trails are built as old ones are overgrown. Places are renamed and the rights to access lakes come and go. The flora and fauna of a particular area move on as new species arrive. Historical facts are distorted with each interpretation, and believe it or not sometimes even lakes disappear (see Heal Lake on page 37).

This book was inspired by curiosity and a desire to learn about the natural world that surrounds us. Use it to experience these places for yourself, and tell your friends about them.

Disclaimers & Warnings

Activities described in this book such as swimming, boating, and hiking each carry their own degree of risk. The author, publisher, and distributor of this book are not responsible for any injury or hardship sustained as a result of reading the material within this book or decisions made based on its content.

Before you head out to the lakes, here are a few specific things to be aware of while you are enjoying the outdoors.

Local Regulations – The lakes in this book are found in provincial parks, regional parks, municipal parks, and even community waterworks. Each lake has its own regulations that must be respected. Each park has different hours, restrictions around pets, and rules for boating activity. While this book gives guidance on policies for access and activities for each lake, it is the responsibility of each person to learn and respect local regulations when visiting them. Always watch for signs on site.

Swimming – The Vancouver Island Health Authority (VIHA) monitors the water quality at the more popular swimming lakes in the area during the summer months. The water quality of lakes in the Victoria area is generally very good for swimming, with the exception of occasional problems at Elk/Beaver Lake due to waterfowl activity. For more information about VIHA's monitoring of lake water visit their website at http://www.viha.ca/mho/water/beach_reports.htm

Drinking Water – Drinking from lakes and streams is not advised as animal and water-fowl feces may cause the drinker to contract Giardia. Some of the sites described in this book will have running water available, but most of them do not. If there is no water supplied and you are not able to take your own water with you, use a fast moving stream or a commercial water filtering product.

Fishing – A valid BC Freshwater Fishing Licence is needed for fishers of 16 or older. Fishing licenses can be purchased online at http://www.fishing.gov.bc.ca/ or in person at different service partners throughout the province.

Boating – Use this book to find places to launch your canoe or kayak, but be aware that only Elk/Beaver and Prospect Lakes allow motorized boats at this time. A boating license is required to operate a motorized vessel in British Columbia. More information on boater licenses can be found at http://www.boaterlicences.com/.

Hiking – There are many trails shown on the maps in this book. Most of the single-track trails do not have signs and are not patrolled. Never hike alone, as even a twisted ankle can leave you immobile. If you arrive at an intersection you are not familiar with, take the larger path. Estimated travel times will be different for each person on any given day. Be conservative and leave early in the day to ensure you have time to get to your destination, enjoy it, and return. Tell someone at home where you plan to go, how you plan to get there, and when you will be back.

Private Land – Some of the shorelines of the lakes featured in this book fall on privately owned land. Respect the wishes of the land owners and do not trespass.

Your Responsibilities

Leave no trace. Not all of the lakes in this book have garbage cans onsite, so bring something you can use to take your garbage out. If you see garbage left by others, pick it up and leave the area better than you found it. Read more about Leave No Trace principles at www.leavenotrace.ca/principles.

Don't feed wildlife. When animals start depending on humans for food they lose their ability to find their own food, and start to seek dangerous interactions with humans.

Stay on the trails. There is life that depends on the ground beneath you. A single footprint can destroy the homes of insects or damage delicate plant life such as moss or wildflowers. Trails have been made for a reason – it is your responsibility to stay on them.

Support the lakes. The lakes that you enjoy today took thousands of years to develop. Human activity over the past hundred years has led to significant deterioration of the ecosystems they support. A list of organizations working to protect, preserve and restore watersheds and ecosystems is included at the back of this book. Please support them. Be aware of what's happening to your lakes and take steps to preserve them.

Lakes 101

Lakes are interesting, living and moving things. Below are answers to a few questions you might have about them.

WHAT IS A LAKE?

The Oxford Dictionary defines as lake as "a large area of water surrounded by land", but beyond that it gets difficult to define what makes up a lake. Some definitions determine a lake by its surface area, while others by its volume. Others will define a lake based on whether it has inflows and outflows (creeks), and still others use the penetration of light to the water's bottom to define a lake.

HOW MANY LAKES ARE THERE IN CANADA?

Canada has around 31,700 large lakes that are over 300 hectares in size, according to data produced by Natural Resources Canada. To put that in context, the largest lake in this book, Elk/Beaver Lake, has a surface area of 246 hectares, meaning none of the lakes in this book are included in that count.

Estimates vary for the total number of lakes in Canada including those below 300 hectares in size, but it is generally accepted that there are between two to three million lakes in Canada, and that Canada has more freshwater lakes than any other country in the world.

WHO OWNS A LAKE?

In most cases the bottom of a lake, the water it holds, and everything in the water are considered public resources. Some lakes are surrounded by privately owned land however, meaning that there is no access to the water for the public. As always there are exceptions to the rule – the bottom of some lakes within the original Esquimalt & Nanaimo (E&N) Land Grant have previously been contested as being privately owned.

WHAT MAKES SOME LAKES WARMER THAN OTHERS?

Sunlight, depth, circulation and elevation are a few of the things that determine the temperature of water in a lake. If you're looking for a warm place to swim, look for beaches on the sunny (north or east) sides of the lakes. Prior Lake is known for its warm water with its low altitude of 66 metres above sea level, yet at 408 metres Grass Lake is plenty warm enough to swim in during the summer months.

WHY ARE SOME LAKES CLEAR AND OTHERS MURKY?

There are three natural factors that affect water clarity. The first is the amount of fine inorganic particulate matter (soil particles) in the water – this is determined by the amount of soil brought into the lake by rain or streams from the surrounding watershed. Algae (microscopic aquatic plants) and can also influence the colour of a lake based on their numbers, and are a natural and vital part of a lake's ecosystem. The third factor is the presence of organic matter, such as decayed vegetation (leaves or needles), also washed into the lake from the surrounding watershed.

Sometimes pollution can also affect the colour of a lake. Whether the lake is fed by a stream or an underground spring it collects everything that rain washes down, and in some cases human waste is pumped directly into a lake. Human development over the past 200 years on land around the lakes has led to runoff from asphalt, septic wastes, fertilizers and household cleaners. This runoff leads to extra nutrients such as phosphorus and nitrogen in lakes, which can sometimes lead to algae blooms.

WHAT MAKES A HEALTHY LAKE?

Lakes must have a sufficient amount of oxygen and nutrients in them to support aquatic life including plants, insects and fish. Cold water can hold more oxygen than warm water. If a lake doesn't have enough oxygen or nutrients in it, or if it has too much of either, sensitive fish such as trout will die. It is difficult to find a lake near Victoria that doesn't have rainbow trout in it, but most of these are stocked, rather than naturally reproducing populations. Langford and Glen Lakes have both had aerations systems installed in them to provide additional oxygen to their water, thereby improving the underwater environment for life in the lake.

Many insects live at the bottom of a lake, some of which can be seen with the naked eye. Insects living in the water are a source of food for fish, crustaceans and other insects. Healthy lakes are generally clear and not noticeably green or tan in colour – cloudy water can clog fish gills and prevent eggs from developing properly.

WHAT ARE THE DIFFERENT KINDS OF LAKES?

There are two ends of the spectrum of lakes – eutrophic and oligotrophic. Lakes that are rich in nutrients such as nitrates and phosphates will usually have plenty of life in them, and are called eutrophic. Oligotrophic lakes on the other hand, have very few nutrients in them, are quite clear but usually sparse in life.

WHAT ARE THE DIFFERENT 'ZONES' OF A LAKE?

From an ecological perspective, lakes are viewed in terms of three different zones: littoral, limnetic and profundal. Littoral refers to the shallow waters near the shore that receive plenty of light and has warm water – this is a good place to watch for small fish, birds, plants or other critters such as salamanders and beavers. The limnetic zone is out past the drop off, where the water is more than eight metres deep. Below eight metres is the profundal zone, where little light reaches, meaning few plants can photosynthesize and produce oxygen.

HOW DOES A LAKE GET ITS NAME?

The name of a lake often reveals its history (such as Prospect Lake), unique natural features of the lake (Grass Lake), or other aspects such as a lake's shape (Spectacle Lake). In British Columbia the names of geographic places, including lakes, are assigned by the Ministry of Natural Resource Operations.

This book tells the history of lake names, but place names continually change. The lakes in this book are more than 12,000 years old, yet they've had their current names for less than 200 years.

WHY DO LAKES MATTER?

Lakes sustain life. From the fish that swim below the surface, to the dragonflies that hunt above, to the birds, critters and animals that inhabit the surrounding forests, life cannot exist without clean water.

Even the 350,000 humans that live in the Capital Regional District would not survive without healthy lakes. The water that flows into their kitchen taps and bath tubs each day originates in Sooke Lake. Lakes matter because they are our access to water, which we simply can't live without.

Aside from the direct physical survival implications of the freshwater lakes provide, there is also an intrinsic, deep human need for access to water for aesthetic, spiritual and artistic reasons.

Historical Context: First Nations and European Settlement

Native peoples have likely lived on what we now call Vancouver Island since the last glaciers melted away over 12,000 years ago.

From smoking fish at "the Smokehouse Lakes" up high in the Sooke Hills, to hunting deer, bear and elk around Thetis Lake and using wood from Cedar trees at Durrance Lake for transportation, clothing and other tools, aboriginal culture supported itself sustainably on freshwater lakes and the ocean for thousands of years.

Then the first European explorers arrived in 1774. The century following the first contact with Europeans saw the population of Salish peoples decimated by European diseases such as small pox, not to mention the veritable robbery of their land.

Between 1850 and 1854 Governor James Douglas negotiated fourteen 'land-sale agreements' with First Nations in and around Fort Victoria and on the north of the Island. In these agreements Douglas traded Hudsons Bay Company blankets for vast swaths of First Nations land. The entire Saanich Peninsula, for example, was "bought" for 386 blankets.

Much of the shoreline on the western side of Grass Lake is wetland.
Photo by Adam Ungstad.

Top Ten: The Best of the Best

One of the great things about a lake is the diversity of things you can do while you are there. The lakes in this book offer a range of activities including swimming, sun tanning, picnicking, paddling, fishing, hiking and even cycling.

What follows are my top picks for the top ten best lakes for each of these activities. Choosing the best lakes for an activity is a difficult task, as all of the lakes offer each activity to some extent, so be sure to check the descriptions for all of the lakes as well as these lists.

Top Ten Best Lakes For Swimming

Durrance (page 33)
Numerous beaches on the north side of the lake and easy access from the main parking lot make Durrance a favourite for swimming and sun. Watch the floating logs for turtles!

Eagles (page 67)
Eagles Lake is a secret swimming hole` tucked away deep in the highlands. Its small size, sand beach and washroom facilities make it a charming place for swimmers of all ages.

Thetis (page 73)
Aside from the two sand beaches to choose from, Thetis Lake has many small access points to ensure there's room for everyone. Even on a busy day it is possible to find a spot for yourself.

Prior (page 79)
The dock at this clothing optional lake is a great place to jump into the refreshing water for a swim. With its small size, low elevation, and plenty of sunshine, Prior Lake is also known for its warm water.

Pease (page 59)
While the crowds are at the larger lakes nearby, choose Pease Lake for a quick swim in the sun. There's no formal beach, but the lake is easy to get into so bring something to float on.

Lookout (page 85)
The sign reading "No Rope Swings Permitted" at the entrance to Colwood's Lookout Lake says it all. Expect a rocky sand beach and plenty of sun.

Glen & Langford (page 93 & 89)
Glen and Langford Lakes both have many beaches and aeration systems have been installed to improve the quality of water and life in the lake.

Spectacle (page 145)
With picnic tables, a good beach, and plenty of sun, Spectacle Lake is a great place to take the family swimming.

Kemp (page 119)
The water in Kemp Lake is some of the clearest and freshest you will find. The beach on the north-east side of the lake is a fantastic place to swim.

Peden (page 139)
This higher elevation lake makes for a great day hike (expect two and a half hours each way) with a refreshing swim waiting to award your efforts in getting there.

Top Ten Best Lakes For Children and Families

Glinz (page 113)
The YMCA-YWCA runs annual summer camps for kids of all ages at Camp Thunderbird, a 1200 acre playground around the crystal clear waters of Glinz Lake.

Swan (page 53)
The Nature House at Swan Lake is not to be overlooked. On a casual visit expect to see live critters such as turtles in the aquariums and be sure to sign up for weekly programming for kids of all ages.

Thetis (page 73)
The main beach has changing facilities, washrooms and picnic tables. The Nature Centre at nearby Francis/King Park also features great programming for kids.

Eagles (page 79)
The sand beach at this small lake is ideal for family picnics on a warm summer afternoon. It also features a unique outhouse with a composting toilet.

Glen (page 93)
Close to the city, with a beach and picnic tables. A carry-in boat launch and fishing pier makes Glen Lake a good place to teach kids to paddle and fish.

Lookout (page 85)
Colwood's Lookout Lake is close to town and has a wide beach area that makes it easy to spread a picnic blanket and watch the kids play in the lake.

Matheson (page 105)
Good parking, a wide sand beach, and washroom facilities make Matheson Lake a favourite for many families.

Spectacle (page 145)
Ample parking, a sandy beach, washrooms and picnic tables. An easy two kilometre trail circles the lake. It is a great place to stop en route to Nanaimo.

Prospect (page 43)
Whitehead Park on the north side of the lake has a beach and playground that are easy to get to from the parking lot.

Langford (page 89)
Langford Lake has many different access points with beaches and picnic tables as well as an easy walking trail along the west side of the lake. Perfect for a day out with the family.

Top Ten Best Lakes For Accessibility

Below are suggestions based on the author's observations for lakes that are accessible to individuals with limited mobility or have difficulty walking.

Durrance (page 33)
An even and well-groomed trail on the north side of Durrance Lake leads from the parking lot to a handful of beaches that make it easy to get in and out of the lake.

Spectacle (page 145)
The main beach at Spectacle Lake is wheelchair accessible from the parking lot, and the two kilometre trail around the lake is even and well-groomed.

Eagles (page 67)
The main beach at Eagles Lake is easy to get to from the parking area, and the slow gradient of the beach makes it easy to get in and out of the water.

Fork (page 63)
A 630 meter loop trail leads from the Munn Road parking lot through lush evergreens, native shrubs, colourful fungi, and wildflowers.

Florence (page 95)
A viewpoint at the north end of the lake is a short walk from the parking area. The sidewalk continues on the east side of the lake to a boardwalk with great views of wetlands on the south side.

Langford (page 89)
The Ed Nixon Trail from Leigh Road to Goldstream Meadows park is a delightful, even trail through trees with accessible viewpoints of the lake. Several access points with beaches are wheelchair accessible.

Elk/Beaver (page 47)
Elk/Beaver Lake offers many even, well-groomed trails around the lake, multiple beaches close to parking, and a wheelchair accessible fishing pier.

Swan (page 53)
The floating boardwalk, view point and Nature House at Swan Lake are wheelchair accessible from the parking lot, making it easy to see the lake and waterfowl who live there.

Blinkhorn (page 101)
Recent improvements to the trail around Blinkhorn Lake make it a very pleasant and easy place to go for a stroll around the lake.

Glinz (page 113)
The trail circling Glinz Lake is an easy walk with interpretive signs, but does pass over some small handmade wooden bridges.

Top Ten Best Lakes For Nature

Peden (page 139)
The moderate to challenging hike to Peden Lake via the wilderness Mary Vine Creek Trail passes by a unique natural feature – waterfalls. Watch for snakes and salamanders in the shallow parts of the lake once you get there.

Glinz (page 113)
The trail that circles Glinz Lake features interpretive signs that highlight the natural features of the lake. Learn about the trees, birds, animals and even insects who call the lake home.

Swan (page 53)
Programs, interpretive displays, and aquariums with live turtles and other critters from the lake offer insight to the natural world at Swan Lake.

Sheilds (page 131)
Regardless of the route the wilderness trails to Sheilds Lake lead through a mid-growth forest of common and not-so-common species native to the area, and the lake itself is full of life.

Crabapple (page 129)
Crabapple Lake is the headwaters of the Charters River, which leads into the Sooke River. Visit the Juan De Fuca Salmon Restoration Society's new interpretive centre at the base of the river (2895 Sooke River Road) on your first visit, then hike to the headwaters of the river on a different visit to find pink water lilies.

Blinkhorn (page 101)
This quiet lake offers a chance to enjoy nature in solitude without requiring a hike into the backcountry. Expect tall trees and sparkling water.

Fork (page 63)
The accessible loop at the Munns Road Entrance leads through impressive mid-growth forest and undergrowth including brilliant moss, colourful mushrooms and wild flowers.

Thetis (page 73)
Despite its popularity and use, Thetis Lake still has some of the most mature forest and best opportunities for getting up close with nature in the area, with plenty of outcrops and hiking trails to explore.

Prior (page 79)
Known for its sunny dock and warm water, Prior Lake offers a chance to enjoy nature in a completely natural state – that is, without clothes.

Elk/Beaver (page 47)
The nature centre near Beaver Beach offers interpretive displays and staff knowledgeable of the area's natural and cultural heritage.

Top Ten Best Lakes For Hiking

Sheilds (page 131)
Sheilds Lake can be reached by two different unmarked, wilderness hikes: up the single track Harrison Trail from Sooke River Rd, or via an old logging road starting at the Harbourview Road trailhead. Expect at least three hours each way.

Peden (page 139)
The unmarked Mary Vine Creek Trail to Peden Lake takes between two to three hours and passes two waterfalls.

Fork (page 63)
Starting from the Munns Road trailhead, follow the summit trail to the top of Mount Work with views of the Saanich Peninsula, and continue down the other side to the parking lot at Ross Durrance Rd.

McKenzie (page 77)
The McKenzie Creek trail branches off the main trail at the north end of Thetis Lake and leads to the southern tip of McKenzie Lake. While access to McKenzie Lake is limited, the trail offers wilderness hiking close to town.

Matheson (page 105)
The trail circling Matheson has two distinct sides – the north side is sunny and relatively level with many access points, while the south side leads uphill through forest and a good view point of the lake below.

Blinkhorn (page 101)
While the trail circling Blinkhorn Lake is an easy walk, a number of single track trails branch off into the woods around the lake.

Thetis (page 73)
Aside from the McKenzie Creek Trail, the north-western tip of Thetis Lake Park contains the little known Bellamy Trail which leads up to Stewart Mountain.

Pease (page 59)
While there are no trails around the shore of Pease Lake, Gowlland Tod park just to the north of the lake offers hiking access to McKenzie Bight with good views of the Finlayson Arm.

Killarney (page 39)
The trail leading from Meadowbrook Road up to Killarney Lake makes for a small but worthwhile hike. The trail leads up a long hill and then circles the lake. There is no parking at Meadowbrook Road, so it's best to arrive on your bike.

Durrance (page 33)
While an easy trail circles Durrance Lake, a network of unmarked wilderness trails lead from the park into the Partridge Hills to the north.

Top Ten Best Lakes For Fishing

Lookout (page 85)
Regularly stocked with rainbow trout, Colwood's Lookout Lake is a favourite for shoreline fishers, float tubes, and even bald eagles looking for some tasty trout.

Spectacle (page 145)
Bring your float tubes, as Spectacle Lake is the one of the very few lakes on Vancouver Island where you'll find Eastern brook trout.

Langford (page 89)
With a large boat launch at Leigh Road it's easy to get on the water at Langford Lake. An aeration system has been installed to improve the quality of the water and life in it.

Elk/Beaver (page 47)
Elk/Beaver lake is one of the few lakes in the area to allow power boats – look for the Brookleigh Boat Launch at the north end. There is also an accessible fishing pier on the west side and plenty of good fishing spots along the trail that circles the lake.

Sheilds (page 131)
If your goal is to spend a quiet afternoon where the only sounds you hear are insects buzzing and fish jumping, start early and make the two to three hour hike up to Sheilds Lake.

Glinz (page 113)
You won't have to wait long to see trout jumping the surface in the fall at Glinz Lake. If you don't have a paddle boat with you, the dock is an ideal place to spend an afternoon fishing.

Glen (page 93)
The fishing pier at the north end of Glen Lake allows for fishing year round, or bring your paddle boat with you in the summer. An aeration system has been installed to improve the water quality in the lake.

Kemp (page 119)
With a carry-in boat launch for non-motorized boats at Chubb Road and very high quality water Kemp Lake is an ideal place to fish from a canoe or other paddle boat.

Prospect (page 43)
Prospect Lake is ideal for fishing from canoes or power boats. The main boat launch is at Echo Drive.

Matheson (page 105)
Matheson offers many points to fish from on the north side of the lake, and boats can be launched from the main beach.

Top Ten Best Lakes For Canoes & Kayaks

Kemp (page 119)
Easy access to launch carry-in boats from Chubb Road or Manatu Road, with plenty of lake to explore. Watch for a nice beach at the north-east end for a great picnic stop.

Thetis (page 73)
The unique shape of Thetis Lake, its islands, cliffs and a culvert between the upper and lower half make it an ideal place to explore with paddle boats.

Peden (page 139)
At an elevation of 316 metres it's a bit of a hike (two to three hours) to get to Peden Lake, but there just might be a canoe waiting for you once you get there!

Durrance (page 33)
Easy access to launch non-motorized boats from the main parking lot, and a generally pleasant place to paddle. Bring your fishing rod.

Glen (page 93)
An enjoyable place to paddle without leaving town. Launch your boat from the north end of the lake.

Langford (page 89)
Unlike its immediate neighbours, a good stretch of Langford Lake is undeveloped providing for a nice shoreline to paddle by, or stop for a picnic lunch on one of the islands in the lake.

Florence (page 95)
The quietest of the lakes in Langford. The boat launch is at the north end, with access from Florence Lake Road.

Matheson (page 105)
Access to the lake is a bit of a walk from the main parking lot, but the shoreline on the far end of Matheson Lake consists mostly of cliffs, making it an ideal place to explore by boat.

Elk/Beaver (page 47)
The rowing centre at Elk/Beaver Lake is an ideal place to learn to paddle. Beaver Lake is quiet with a variety of shorelines, wetlands and islands to explore.

Spectacle (page 145)
Easy access to launch a paddle boat at the main beach, but expect to carry your boat a small distance.

Top Ten Best Lakes For Dogs

Killarney (page 39)
There is a great walking trail for dogs from Meadowbrook Road, and a good access point to the lake for a dog to chase balls or Frisbees in the water.

Langford (page 89)
The Ed Nixon trail, particularly in Goldstream Meadows Park, is perfect for walking the dogs.

Elk/Beaver (page 47)
With a 10 km trail circling the lake, Elk/Beaver Lake is a great place for taking the dogs for an afternoon walk.

Thetis (page 73)
A longstanding favourite for dogs and their owners. Park at the second beach as it is the best place to let your dog get into the water.

Blinkhorn (page 101)
Your dog will love the even path that circles this quiet beauty in the heart of Metchosin. A good lake for dogs as it has interesting trails and gets fewer swimmers than some of the other lakes close by.

Kemp (page 119)
The boat launch area at Chubb Road is a favourite swimming hole for dogs. Bring a tennis ball. The trail at Manatu Road is also an interesting place to explore with your pooch.

Matheson (page 107)
Matheson Lake has a network of trails in the surrounding hills, and the trail circling the lake has a few access points, other than then main beach, that are suitable for letting dogs into the water.

Fork (page 63)
The trail leading from the Munn Road Parking lot is a fantastic place for dogs, but be sure to keep them on the trail as much of the undergrowth in this area consists of fragile mushrooms, wildflowers and mosses.

Spectacle (page 145)
The trail that circles Spectacle Lake features several places suitable to let a dog get in the water.

Prospect (page 43)
While it doesn't have an extensive trail network, Whitehead Park is a suitable place to play fetch with dogs during the off season (dogs are prohibited at the beach between May 1 – August 31).

Top Ten Best Lakes For Bicycles

BICYCLE DAY TRIPS

Matheson (page 105)
About 32 kilometres from town by the Galloping Goose Regional Trail, Matheson Lake is a great cycling destination for those looking to make a day out of it. Watch for a sign off the main trail leading directly to the main parking lot, or continue down the Goose for other access points.

Killarney (page 39)
You will feel very smug cycling down Meadowbrook Road knowing that there is no parking for cars at the end. Leave the Galloping Goose Trail at Burnside Road West and follow Prospect Lake Road until you see Meadowbrook Road to your left.

Thetis (page 73)
Start with Thetis Lake for your first day trip by bike. Follow the Galloping Goose Trail and exit at the bridge that crosses Six Mile Road – watch for the sign. When you get to the main beach follow the road to the left and lock up at the bike rack at the second beach so you can explore the upper half of Thetis.

Blinkhorn (page 101)
Blinkhorn Lake is a good alternative to Matheson if you'd like to avoid the crowds. Exit the Galloping Goose at Lindholm for a good climb (and fun descent afterwards) or at Kangaroo Road if hills aren't your thing.

Pease (page 59)
Cycling in the highlands is very different from riding on the trails or in the city. Count on winding, narrow roads leading through dense forests and hills. Take it easy and keep an eye out for cars coming around the next corner. Pease Lake is a good distance away and an interesting ride for experienced cyclists.

MOUNTAIN BIKING

Durrance (page 33)
Durrance Lake is close to Mount Work Park which has plenty of mountain biking trails, but the Partridge Hills directly to the North of Durrance Lake are also a good place to learn to mountain bike.

Sheilds (page 131)
Mountain biking is a great way to get to Sheilds Lake as it will make your return much faster than your ascent. Choose the access from Harbourview Road if it's your first time there, or for those familiar with the area use the Harrison Trail to get up to Grass Lake.

Killarney (page 39)
Directly to the east of the mountain biking trails at Mount Work Park, Killarney Lake is a great place to go for a swim after a day on the trails.

Glinz (page 113)
The network of trails through the forest around Glinz Lake are ideal for mountain biking.

Kemp (page 119)
To the east of Kemp Lake is Broom Hill, a favourite for mountain bikers. From Otter Point Road turn onto Burr Road, then left onto Petemar, and right onto Blanchard. Look for parking at the end of Blanchard Street.

Opposite: Prospect Lake as seen from South Prospect Lake Park. Photo by Adam Ungstad.

Saanich

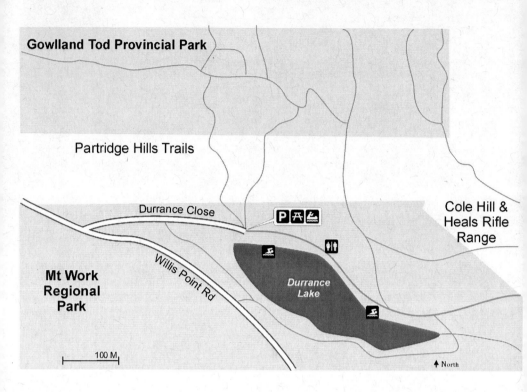

Gowlland Tod Provincial Park

Partridge Hills Trails

Durrance Close

Cole Hill &
Heals Rifle
Range

**Mt Work
Regional
Park**

Willis Point Rd

*Durrance
Lake*

100 M

↑ North

Durrance Lake

Durrance Lake is one of the best places to soak up sun and enjoy a beach atmosphere near Victoria. The trail that circles the lake is flat and wide on the north side, offering access to strollers and wheelchairs.

FACTS

Surface Area	8 ha
Max Depth	16 m
Elevation	134 m
Land Status	Regional Park

ACTIVITIES

Swimming	Good swimming. Watch for turtles.
Hiking	Easy 2 km trail circles the lake, with unmarked trails branching off into the Partridge Hills to the north.
Cycling	Partridge Hills to the north and Mount Work Park to the south are ideal for mountain biking.
Boating	Car-top boat launch from the main beach. Electric-motors only.
Fishing	Popular for fly fishing. Expect to find smallmouth bass, rainbow trout (stocked in 2012) and cutthroat trout.
Picnics	Picnic tables at the main beach.
Pets	Must be on leash passing through beach areas.

FACILITIES

Beach	Several sandy beaches on the north shore.
Washrooms	Available at the main parking lot.
Accessibility	Trail along the north side of the lake is wheelchair accessible. The south side is narrow and twisted but not difficult.

Fishing at Durrance Lake in the fall. Photo by Adam Ungstad.

DIRECTIONS FROM VICTORIA

1. *Head north on Douglas St (Trans-Canada Hwy)*

2. *Turn right onto Bay St*

4. *Turn left onto Blanshard St (Patricia Bay Hwy)*

5. *Take Exit 9 for Quadra Street toward Saanich Road W*

6. *Turn left onto Quadra St*

7. *Continue onto W Saanich Rd*

8. *Turn left onto Wallace Dr*

9. *Turn left onto Willis Point Rd*

10. *Turn right onto Durrance Rd*

The largest lake in Mount Work Park, Durrance Lake is best known for the beaches that dot the northern side of its shore, and rightfully so - this is a great place to soak up some sun! The easy access to the water, parking, and washroom facilities also make Durrance Lake an ideal place to spend an afternoon with the family.

From the parking lot the wide, well-groomed gravel trail leads immediately to the sunny and open north side of the lake, passing washroom facilities. If the first beach is too busy, walk a little further to the next one. If that one is too busy, continue and you'll find several more beaches and access points, providing plenty of space for everyone to enjoy this natural beauty.

Following the lake around the west side, the two kilometer trail changes into a narrow, twisting path that continues around the shady south side of the lake. Here the trees go right to the waters edge but the occasional fallen log provides an alternate entry to the lake for swimmers looking to avoid the crowds of the beaches on the north side.

From the north side of the lake you can access a series of unmarked and unmaintained trails up to the Partridge Hills, a favourite for mountain biking.

If you are walking the trail in late March, watch for western white trillium, a white flower with three petals that turns pink or purple as it reaches the end of their lifespan in May. With the lack of wind in the area the trillium relies on the hardworking ants below to find new homes for their seeds.

A variety of trees can be found along the trail, including arbutus, grand fir, douglas fir, red alders, and cedar. Red alders are often the first trees to establish themselves after a forest fire or logging, indicating that some of the land surrounding Durrance Lake has been previously disturbed.

Be sure to watch for birds such as Steller's jay, woodpeckers, and hummingbirds in the area, feeding on insects and berries produced by the surrounding ecosystem.

Did you know?

The summit trail leaving from the parking lot on Ross Durrance Rd leads to the top of Mount Work through a grove of arbutus trees and raven nesting areas. At 449 meters high, this peak is the highest point on the Saanich Peninsula and offers panoramic views of the area including Gowland Tod Provincial Park, Thetis Lake, Prospect Lake, Victoria, and even the Olympic Mountains in Washington State.

The trail is considered moderate to challenging, so bring a friend, proper clothes, and lunch. Continuing down the south side of the mountain will take you to the quiet Fork Lake in the heart of the highlands.

A western painted turtle soaks up the sun at Durrance Lake. Photo by Carly Macoun.

HISTORY

In 1960 the City of Victoria acquired the land around Durrance Lake from BC Electric in a trade: 204 acres of land around Durrance Lake in exchange for 105 acres of land directly north of Thetis Lake. The 105 acres of Thetis Lake Park were needed by BC Electric to build power lines into the city.

Did you know?

If you have trouble spelling the word "Durrance" you're not the only one – the name of this lake has a history of different spellings. Named after pioneering settlers in the area, the name was first recorded as "Durant" by the Geological Survey in 1911, followed by "Durants" on Hibben's Map in 1929, "Durrant" by the BC Gazetteer in 1930, and finally as "Durrance" in 1934 by the Saanich Municipality.

Heal Lake

Heal Lake is a ghost.

It was drained by the Capital Regional District in 1991 to make additional space for the Hartland Regional Landfill. What do you think you'd find at the bottom of a drained lake that was formed by a glacier thousands of years ago?

Believe it or not, logs. Hundreds of perfectly preserved logs, some of which are nearly 10,000 years old were found in the sediments at the bottom of Heal Lake.

These logs have been studied by researchers from the University of Victoria, creating insight into historical climatic events of Vancouver Island. The logs have rings for each year old they are, and the research on those rings shows that a tidal wave hit this coast shortly after the glaciers melted.

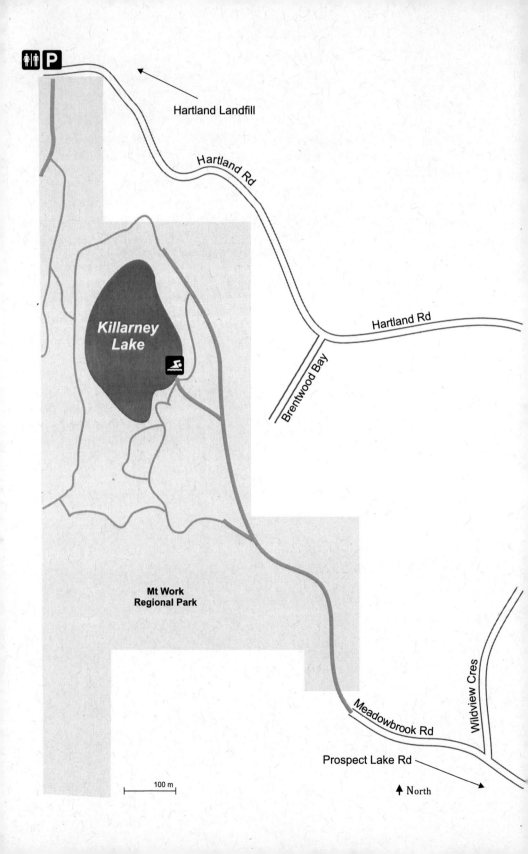

Killarney Lake

A beautiful, healthy, hidden delight in the heart of the Sannich Peninsula. A great destination for a day trip for experienced cyclists.

FACTS

Surface Area	4 ha
Max Depth	5 m
Elevation	107 m
Land Status	Regional Park

ACTIVITIES

Swimming	Good swimming.
Hiking	Access from Meadowbrook Rd is a moderate uphill walk to the trail circling the lake.
Cycling	Mountain biking opportunities in Mt Work Park – trails are immediately to the west of the lake.
Boating	No access.
Picnics	No picnic tables, but the main beach is ideal for a picnic lunch.
Pets	Must be under control and on trails.

FACILITIES

Beach	Easy access to the water but no sand beach.
Washrooms	None.
Accessibility	Not wheelchair accessible.

At the end of Meadowbrook Road, Killarney Lake is an ideal destination for cyclists.
Photo by Adam Ungstad.

DIRECTIONS FROM VICTORIA

1. *Head north on Douglas St (Trans-Canada Hwy)*

2. *Take Exit 8 toward View Royal*

3. *Merge onto Helmcken Rd N*

4. *Turn left onto Burnside Rd W*

5. *Turn right onto Prospect Lake Rd*

6. *Slight right to stay on Prospect Lake Rd*

7. *Turn left onto Meadowbrook Rd*

8. *Park on Wildview Crescent*

Killarney Lake has two distinct sides to it and people approaching the lake from different directions will see two very different lakes.

Approaching from the south by the trail from Meadowbrook Road is a unique, unforgettable experience. The rural road leads past farms and cabins before it becomes a walking trail at the end. There is no parking at the trail head, so the best access is by bike or on foot.

After a 15-20 minute hike with some steep hills you come to a picture-perfect clearing on the shore of Killarney Lake, with a rock perfect for a picnic, and easy walk-in access to the lake just below. It is quite a beautiful place.

On the other hand, approaching from the north yields a different lake altogether. While most of the shoreline of Killarney Lake is part of Mount Work Park (a favourite for mountain bikers), a small portion of the shoreline is private property. To further complicate things, a BC Hydro right-of-way borders the lake on its west side, and the Hartland landfill is a short distance to the north. You can access the lake from the BC Hydro right-of-way, but it will require a small amount of bush-whacking as there is no formal trail.

Despite its proximity to the landfill and power lines, Killarney Lake is full of life and is a treasure to those who know about it. The Capital Regional District (CRD) has programs in place to monitor the quality of ground and surface water near the Hartland Landfill, and Killarney Lake has consistently met provincial guidelines for water quality.

Beaver activity in recent years has caused fluctuations in the lake's level and a few drowned cedar trees, so keep an eye out for beavers hard at work while you are there.

HISTORY

Killarney Lake was originally known as Surprise Lake. A mapping error then mislabelled it as Mud Lake, a name that was intended for a pond nearby.

In a 1928 letter to the Geographic Board, the owner of land around the lake, Herbert F. Shade, stated that he had changed the name to "Killarney" but as there were two other lakes in BC with the same name asked for his to be listed as "Lake Kilarney" – removing an 'l' from the name.

The Geographic Board rejected the request for the spelling change, and suggested "Shade Lake" instead. Mr. Shade declined the offer out of respect for his business partner, and the lake today continues to be known as "Killarney Lake."

To this day there are still three Killarney Lakes in British Columbia – the second is found on the nearby Bowen Island, and the third in the far north of the mainland.

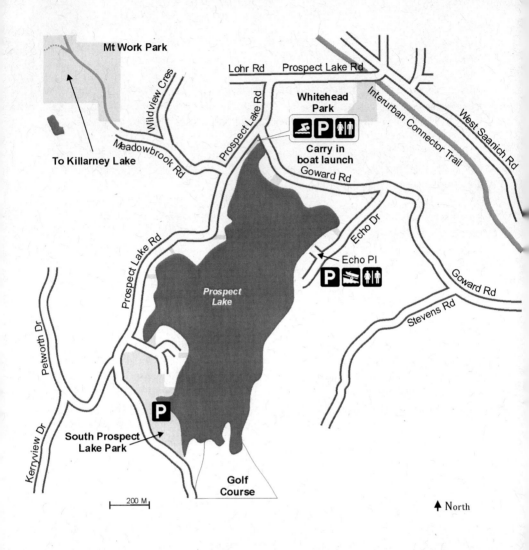

Prospect Lake

Opportunities for picnics, boating, fishing, bird watching, and even golfing in the Saanich Peninsula.

FACTS

Surface Area	65 ha
Max Depth	14 m
Elevation	48 m
Land Status	Municipal Parks / Private Land

ACTIVITIES

Swimming	Good swimming. Beach at Whitehead Park.
Hiking	Some short trails at South Prospect Lake Park.
Cycling	Access via Interurban Connector Trail.
Boating	Boat-trailer access at Echo Drive, carry-in boat access at Whitehead Park and Estelline Park.
Fishing	Rainbow and cutthroat trout (stocked 2012).
Picnics	Playground and picnic tables at Whitehead park suitable for a family afternoon well spent, as well as a more secluded view point on the shore at South Prospect Lake Park.
Pets	Must be on a leash.

FACILITIES

Beach	Sand beach at Whitehead Park.
Washrooms	Available at Whitehead Park and Echo Drive.
Accessibility	Whitehead Park is wheelchair accessible.

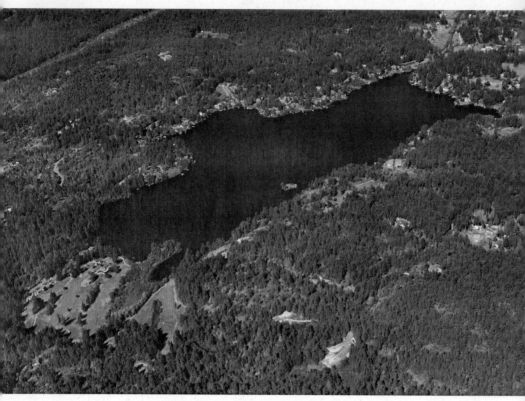

An aerial view of Prospect Lake shows the golf course at the south end.
Photo courtesy of the Prospect Lake Golf Course.

DIRECTIONS FROM VICTORIA

1. *Head north on Douglas St (Trans-Canada Hwy)*

2. *Take Exit 8 toward View Royal*

3. *Merge onto Helmcken Rd N*

4. *Turn left onto Burnside Rd W*

5. *Turn right onto Prospect Lake Rd*

While most of the shoreline around Prospect Lake has been claimed by private residences, there are two small parks and a boat launch that provide access for the public. Boats with electric motors are permitted on the lake with speed restrictions and can be launched at Echo Drive. Rainbow trout and cutthroat bass are stocked regularly.

On the north end is Whitehead Park, which features a small playground. Recent efforts have been made by volunteers and the District of Saanich to improve the playground and restore the creek bed that borders the park.

The south end of the lake holds the secluded South Prospect Lake Park, a mostly wooded area that leads to the rocky water's edge below via a series of short, somewhat steep trails. Watch for birds such as chickadees, nuthatches, sparrows, and flickers on your way. Next to the park is the Prospect Lake Golf Course where you can play a round of nine holes and enjoy a view of the lake from the patio. The golf course was built by Andrew and Dot McGregor in 1964.

The history of Prospect Lake shows the impact that human settlement can have on an ecosystem in a very short time. In 1956 the water in the lake was declared unfit for drinking, and water was then brought to the surrounding homes through an expansion of the Capital Regional District's water supply system. A report submitted to Saanich Council in 2002 stated that staphylococcus was present in the lake, indicating that sewage was a significant source of contamination. A Beach Report issued by the Vancouver Island Health Authority in September 2011 states that Prospect Lake is safe for swimming.

HISTORY

Prospect Lake likely took its name from the forty-niners (a reference to the year of 1849) who came from California in search of gold. While there is no evidence that gold was ever found in the area, the name Prospect Lake stuck even after the prospectors moved on.

Whitehead Park is named after the Whitehead family, who sold the land to Saanich in 1959. Herbert Thomas Whitehead was an architect from England who designed an elaborate house at the corner of Cook Street and Dallas Road in Victoria. The house, built in 1913, is now an elegant Bed and Breakfast known as the Dashwood Manor.

The community of Prospect Lake has a rich history full of stories and fascinating trivia. For more information about the history of the lake, find a copy of *Reflections on Prospect Lake*, a book produced by the Prospect Lake Heritage Society in 2012.

Did you know?
One of the first settlers of Prospect Lake was On Hing, a hard working Chinese man who arrived in 1858 and owned 89 acres of land on the southeast side of the lake. On Hing, his wife, and family planted strawberries and fruit orchards over most of their land. On Hing was known as a happy individual who travelled around the countryside with his wagon full of produce and chickens, trading for fresh meat, grain, and other supplies. Other than the work done cultivating their land and raising their family, little is known about On Hing's wife.

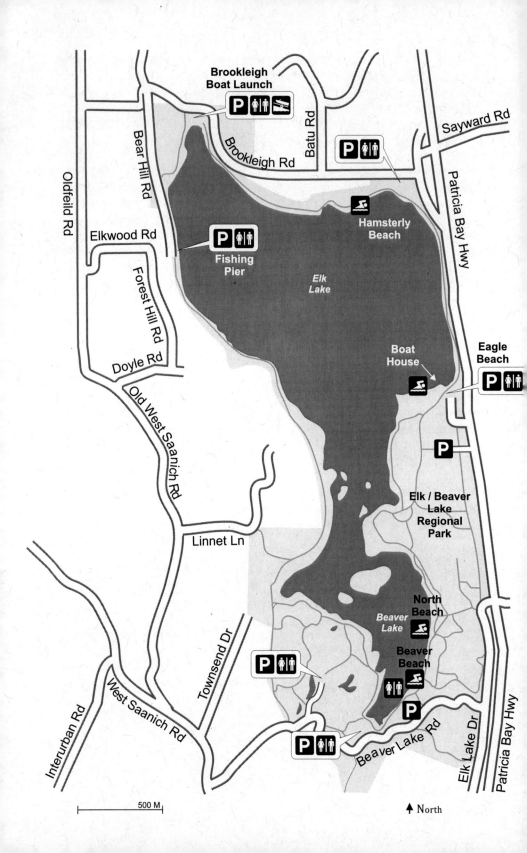

Elk/Beaver Lake

Elk/Beaver Lake is the largest lake in the Victoria area with opportunities for paddling, rowing, hiking, fishing, and swimming. The lake has excellent facilities including two sand beaches, a boat launch, a fishing platform, and a 2.5-hour accessible trail along the shoreline.

FACTS

Surface Area	246 ha
Max Depth	19 m
Elevation	65 m
Land Status	Regional Park

ACTIVITIES

Swimming   Beaches are sometimes closed for swimming at Elk/Beaver lake due to waterfowl activity. Watch for signs onsite or contact the Vancouver Island Health Authority at (250) 370-8699.

Hiking   An easy 10 km trail circles the lake.

Cycling   Access via Lochside Trail & Haliburton Rd. Cycling permitted on some multi-use trails.

Boating   Carry-in boat launch at Eagle Beach. Motorized boat launch at Brookleigh Boat Launch. Power boats permitted in the northwest corner of the lake only.

Fishing   Rainbow trout (stocked 2012).

Picnics   Picnic tables and facilities throughout the park.

Pets   Must be under control and on trails. Dogs must be on a leash when passing through beach areas.

Canadian geese enjoying the water at Beaver Lake. Photo by Mike J Munroe.

FACILITIES

Beach	Three sand beaches: Beaver, Eagles, and Hamsterly.
Washrooms	Available at all beaches and primary access points.
Accessibility	Most of the 10 km lakeside trail is even and wheelchair accessible. Highlights include an accessible fishing pier on the west side of the lake.

DIRECTIONS FROM VICTORIA

1. *Head north on Douglas St (Trans-Canada Hwy)*

2. *Turn right onto Bay St*

3. *Turn left onto Blanshard St (Patricia Bay Hwy)*

4. *Continue to follow Patricia Bay Hwy/BC-17 N*

5. *Turn left onto Elm Lake Dr / Haliburton Rd*

6. *Turn left onto Elk Lake Dr*

Elk/Beaver Lake is often a visitor's first impression of Vancouver Island as they glimpse its sparkling blue waters from the Patricia Bay Highway en route from the airport or Swartz Bay ferry terminal to Victoria. Its size, wide range of amenities and general accessibility ensure that Elk Lake has something to offer everyone.

The lake and surrounding wetlands attract birds such as mergansers, buffleheads, mallards, geese, and eagles, and the vegetation along the shoreline provides homes for river otter, western painted and the endangered red-eared slider turtles.

Elk Lake is also one of the premier places to fish in the area. The lake is stocked each year with rainbow trout and is known for having a healthy population of 3-4 pound smallmouth bass. Many anglers have taken up the sport of fly-fishing for these feisty fish at Elk/Beaver Lake.

Hamsterly Beach on the north side is a large, car accessible sand beach that gets plenty of sunshine and is perfect for swimmers and picnickers. Beaver Beach also offers access to the lake on the south side.

The easy trail around the lake takes about 2.5 hours to complete and leads through forests of Douglas fir and western red cedar. Watch out for bald eagles and osprey hunting for fish in the lake.

Being the largest lake in the area, Elk Lake is naturally a favourite for rowers. A variety of rowing programs are offered for athletes of all ages by the Victoria City Rowing Club at the boathouse just off the highway. Watch for regattas hosted by the University of Victoria's rowing club and other local rowing organizations.

Elk Lake is known for its polar bear swims that take place on New Year's Day each year. Talk about getting a fresh start!

Elk/Beaver Lake in the spring. Photo by Mike J Munroe.

HISTORY

Elk Lake once served as Victoria's primary water supply. In 1864 the Spring Ridge Water Company laid log pipes to transport water from the Elk Lake to downtown Victoria. Families would either go downtown to fill their water barrels, or have the water delivered to them by horse and wagon. In 1875 water from Elk Lake began to be piped directly to Victoria homes.

The city grew quickly in this period, so the level of Beaver Lake was raised in 1895 to connect it with Elk Lake, thereby increasing the water supply. The current name of Elk/Beaver Lake Park serves as a reminder that this lake was once two separate bodies of water.

Pieces of this era can still be seen in the double track trail on the west side of the lake that used to be part of a railway offering service between Victoria and Sidney from 1894 to 1919.

As one might expect, Elk and Beaver Lakes were named after animals who enjoyed the lakes. While elk are not present on the Saanich Peninsula today, they can still be found in the Sooke area from time to time.

Did you know?
The Beaver Lake Store, currently at 4808 West Saanich Road, started as a small confectionery on the east side of the road, but cousins Eulalie and Marie Harrison literally hauled the building across the street when their landlord raised the rent. They later rented and purchased the property where the store currently stands.

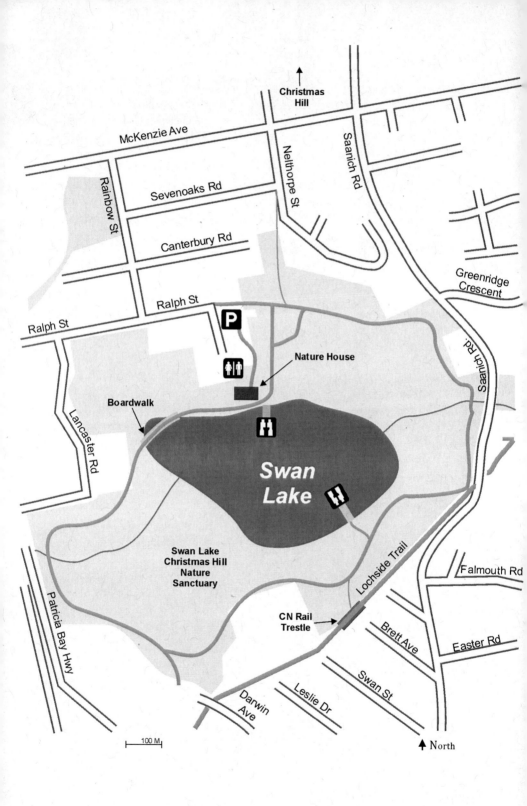

Swan Lake

Swan Lake is a thriving nature sanctuary in Victoria's suburban backyard. Not only does it boast a wide variety of plants, animals, birds, and insects, it also has great walking trails, a floating boardwalk, and an interpretive Nature House to help you explore the nature of the area.

FACTS

Surface Area	9 ha
Max Depth	7 m
Elevation	12 m
Land Status	Nature Sanctuary

ACTIVITIES

Swimming   Swimming not permitted. The lake and surrounding area are designated as a Nature Sanctuary, and as such the water is reserved as a refuge for waterfowl. Wetlands surround the lake, resulting in a muddy bottom unpleasant for swimming.

Hiking   Easy walking trails around the lake with an optional hike to Christmas Hill, a Garry Oak preserve to the north of the lake.

Cycling   Access from the Lochside trail. No bikes in the park.

Boating   No access.

Picnics   Floating viewpoints and boardwalks with benches are ideal for a picnic lunch.

Pets   Pets are not permitted at Swan Lake.

The floating boardwalk at Swan Lake. Photo by the Swan Lake Christmas Hill Nature Sanctuary.

FACILITIES

Beach	None.
Washrooms	Available at the Nature House.
Accessibility	Some lakeside trails and the floating boardwalk are wheelchair accessible.

DIRECTIONS FROM VICTORIA

1. *Head north on Douglas St (Trans Canada Hwy)*

2. *Turn right onto Bay St*

3. *Turn left onto Blanshard St (Patricia Bay Hwy)*

4. *Take Exit 7 for Mckenzie Avenue toward Nanaimo / Sooke*

6. *Keep right at the fork, follow signs for University Of Victoria and merge onto McKenzie Ave*

7. *Turn right onto Rainbow St*

8. *Turn left onto Ralph St*

9. *Take the 1st right onto Swan Lake Rd*

The Nature House at Swan Lake, run by the Swan Lake Christmas Hill Nature Sanctuary, features aquariums with painted turtles and lizards as well as a reading room with an impressive collection of books on the flora and fauna of the Victoria area. It features a Native Plant Garden with interpretative information, in addition to bird watching programs. Don't miss the Valentine's Day Couple's Bird Watch!

The shores of Swan Lake are a marshy habitat with cattails and duckweed providing food and refuge for a wide variety of waterfowl as well as muskrats, river otters, and mink. The trees surrounding the lake are inhabited by wrens, warblers, and other song birds. Great-horned owls and peregrines can sometimes be seen above, hunting over the marsh.

Of course, where there are birds, there must be insects. Buzzing across the water and through the marsh of Swan Lake are damselflies, dragonflies, water beetles, and water striders. These insects also provide food for the resident newts and frogs.

In addition to the fauna of the lake you'll find unique flora and fungi. Look for Garry oak, arbutus, and Douglas fir trees, along with some of the oldest heritage cottonwood trees in the region.

If you are a fungi enthusiast, watch for the Annual Mushroom Show hosted by the South Vancouver Island Mycological Society in late October each year. In the winter, Swan Lake is also a great place to be after a snowfall, where you can find tracks in the snow left by critters such as muskrats and mink.

The trail around the lake and surrounding marsh is an easy 30-40 minute walk, highlighted by the floating boardwalk a short distance from the Nature House. On your walk notice the shape of the surrounding hills and the vegetation that inhabits the marshes, which indicate that the lake used to be larger than its current form.

If you're looking for a longer walk, visit the Garry oak preserve on the nearby Christmas Hill where you'll find butterflies, wildflowers, and vistas of the surrounding area.

While its location makes Swan Lake accessible for an afternoon stroll, human settlement around the lake hasn't been without drawbacks. Swan Lake has often been under threat from run-off and other forms of human pollution from the nearby hills. This pollution has caused nitrogen levels in the lake to rise, resulting in the algae often seen on the fringes of the lake.

HISTORY

Before it was a nature sanctuary, Swan Lake had a history in hospitality. In 1864 the Swan Lake Hotel was constructed on its south side. Guests could fish in the summer, skate in the winter, and dance all year long at the hotel until it burned to ground thirty years later. The Hotel was rebuilt, but consumed by fire again three years later in 1897.

Opposite: The accessible loop trail at Fork Lake leads through tall mid-growth forest.
Photo by Adam Ungstad

Highlands

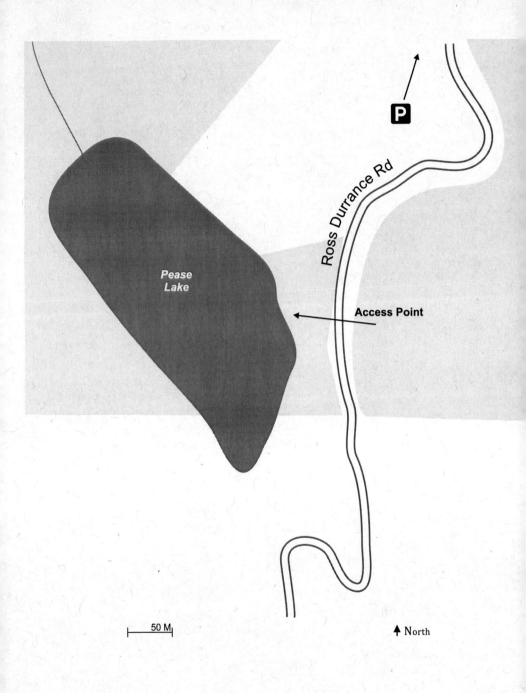

Pease
Lake

Ross Durrance Rd

P

Access Point

50 M

↑ North

Pease Lake

Found in the north-west corner of Mount Work Park, the quiet and little-known Pease Lake is an ideal destination for swimmers and cyclists.

FACTS

Surface Area	3.8 ha
Max Depth	6.5 m
Elevation	139 m
Land Status	Regional Park / Private Land

ACTIVITIES

Swimming	Good swimming. Watch for turtles.
Hiking	No hiking trails at the lake, but plenty of trails nearby in Mount Work Park and Gowlland Tod Park. Watch for the trailheads further up Ross Durrance Road.
Cycling	Access via the narrow and winding Millstream Lake Rd or by the Interurban Connector Trail and Willis Pt Rd.
Boating	Carry-in boats only. No parking for a boat trailer however.
Fishing	Best suited for float tubes, as there is no shoreline fishing and limited access to launch carry-in boats.
Picnics	None.
Pets	Must be under control and on trails.

FACILITIES

Beach	Good access to the water, but no sand beach.
Washrooms	Available at the entrance to Mount Work Park.
Accessibility	Easy wheelchair access to the water but no parking.

Pease Lake, a secret swimming hole just to the west of Durrance Lake.
Photo by Adam Ungstad.

DIRECTIONS FROM VICTORIA

1. *Head north on Douglas St (Trans-Canada Hwy)*

2. *Turn right onto Bay St*

3. *Turn left onto Blanshard St (Patricia Bay Hwy)*

4. *Take Exit 9 for Quadra Street toward Saanich Road W*

5. *Turn left onto Quadra St*

6. *Continue onto W Saanich Rd*

7. *Turn left onto Wallace Dr*

8. *Turn left onto Willis Point Rd*

9. *Turn left onto Ross Durrance Rd*

10. *Park at entrance to Mount Work Park*

Largely surrounded by Douglas fir and cedar trees, Pease Lake is a quiet, little known beauty found at the fringes of Mount Work Park. Pease Lake is particularly well-suited for cyclists, as the nearest parking lot is further up Durrance Road at the entrance to the park. Trees and a handful of private homes surround most of the shoreline, so it's best to count on being in the water for this one. Bring a float-tube if you are fishing or an air mattress if you are swimming.

While you are there, watch (or listen) for pacific chorus frogs, also known as pacific tree-frogs. These frogs are native to the area and are unique as they can change the colour of their skin from bright green to brown depending on the temperature and humidity of the air around them. They are also very loud considering their small size of 2 - 5 centimetres. Watch for red-eared slider turtles at Pease Lake as well.

There are no trails circling the lake, but there are plenty of walking and hiking trails in Gowlland Tod Park just to the north. These trails will take you to a rocky beach on the McKenzie Bight (of the Saanich Inlet) with good views of the Finlayson Arm. Look for the trailhead across the road from the Ross Durrance Road parking lot for Mount Work Park.

HISTORY

The son of immigrants from Scotland, Duncan Ross moved from Ontario to the Victoria area in 1890 and worked as a school teacher in Vic West. While exploring the woods in the Saanich Highlands, as the area was known then, he came across Pease Lake and subsequently bought 160 acres of land in the area and built a small log cabin at the lake.

An enterprising individual, Mr. Ross left Victoria shortly afterwards to improve his financial status by opening a newspaper in the booming mining town of Greenwood in the interior of B.C. He married his wife, Birdie Thomson, in Greenwood and together they moved to Ottawa after he was elected as a member of parliament. Following several other pursuits, including a role in the construction of a portion of the Grand Trunk Railway near Hazelton, Mr. Ross returned to Victoria in 1910 to build a home for his wife and three daughters on Rockland Avenue.

By 1913 the family had built several extensions to the original log cabin at Pease Lake, and proceeded to open "Ross Ranch." At the time the only route to the ranch was a dirt road leading from Langford, which ended at their front door. Duncan Ross died in 1916, and by 1918 Birdie decided that her family would live at the ranch full time. Victoria writer Bob McMinn has written many colourful accounts of life at the ranch for the Highlander, a newsletter issued by the Highlands District Community Association.

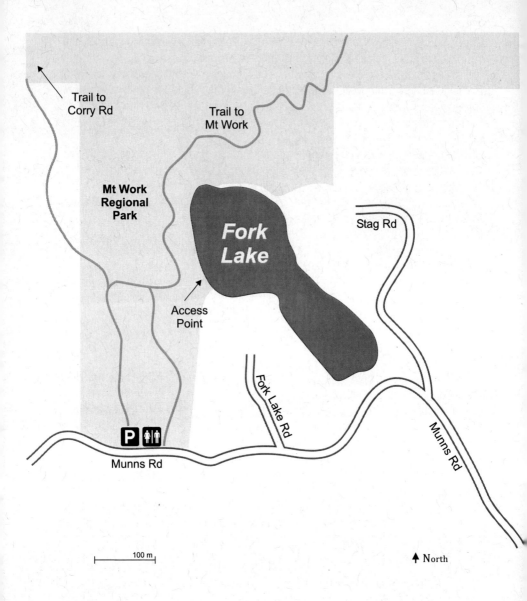

Fork Lake

At the south end of Mount Work Park, Fork Lake offers a pleasant opportunity to stroll through tall evergreens and admire the natural beauty of the Highlands. Watch your step, as native moss, fungi and wildflowers abound.

FACTS

Surface Area	3 ha
Max Depth	10 m
Elevation	216 m
Land Status	Regional Park / Private Land

ACTIVITIES

Swimming	Yes, but no easy access to the water.
Hiking	Accessible 630 m walking loop on the west side of the lake. 11 km moderate to challenging hiking trail continues from north end of the lake to the top of Mt. Work and down the other side to Ross Durrance Rd.
Cycling	Access via Munn Rd. Cycling prohibited in the park.
Boating	No access.
Fishing	Best suited for float tubes, as there is no shoreline fishing and limited access to launch carry-in boats.
Picnics	None.
Pets	Must be under control and on trails.

FACILITIES

Beach	None.
Washrooms	Available at Munn Rd parking lot.
Accessibility	A fully accessible 630 m loop trail starts at from Munn Rd parking lot and takes a clockwise route through ferns, shrubs, mosses, and wild woodland flowers.

Watch the ground for many types of mushrooms at Fork Lake. Photo by Adam Ungstad.

DIRECTIONS FROM VICTORIA

1. *Head north on Douglas St (Trans-Canada Hwy)*

2. *Take Exit 8 toward View Royal*

3. *Merge onto Helmcken Rd N*

4. *Turn left onto Burnside Rd W*

5. *Turn right onto Prospect Lake Rd*

6. *Turn left onto Munns Rd*

While Fork Lake isn't ideal for swimming, it is a perfect place to connect with the natural world. In particular, pay attention to the ground on your visit to Fork Lake, where you'll find a fascinating variety of fungi, deep mosses, and wildflowers. Be sure to stay on the trail of course, as human feet are unaware of their own power and are apt to destroy these beauties without realizing what they are trampling over.

While residences are found on the east side of Fork Lake, the west side falls within the Mount Work Regional Park and serves as the trail head for a hike up to the summit of Mount Work. While you may catch a glimpse of the lake now and then from the trail, actual access to the water is severely limited and requires wading through bushes.

Following the trail from the parking lot at Munn Road around the west shore of Fork Lake you will reach a fork in the path – continuing to the right leads up to the summit of Mount Work, and another largely unknown historical feature, Corry Road, is to the left.

Corry Road was built in the 1920s to connect families living at Fork Lake with their neighbours living at Third Lake and connects Munn Road to Ross Durrance Road

Today the road falls mostly within public rights of way (approximately 300 meters of the road are on private land) and offers an accessible and relatively easy trail within a biologically complex and diverse ecosystem.

The largely undisturbed second-growth forest Corry Road passes through enables visitors to appreciate the beauty of the natural world, and is enjoyed for photography, bird-watching, and outdoor art creation.

Accessible Loop Trail

Fork Lake features an accessible 630-metre loop trail that leads through tall evergreens and rich undergrowth. Start at the Munn Road entrance, and take a clockwise route.

HISTORY

Built in 1910, the Fork Lake Ditch is considered a symbol of the pioneer drive to not only survive but also to move beyond subsistence.

Found on the west side of the lake, the ditch was dug and blasted by an early property owner named Frank Gregory. Gregory had determined that by lowering the level of the lake he would be able to create more land for grazing for his livestock.

Indeed, he was right – the ditch allowed water from Fork Lake to drain into Fizzle Lake to the south, reducing the level of Fork Lake by nearly ten feet and creating 7000 square meters of new land for his livestock.

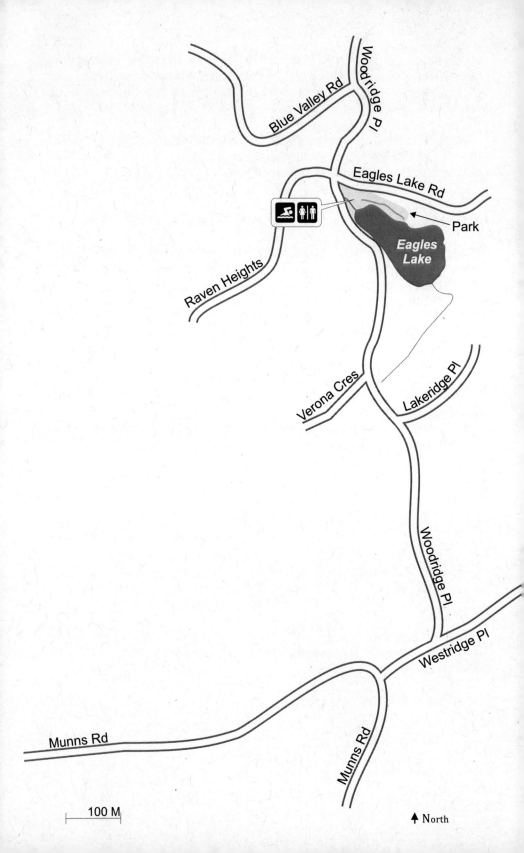

Eagles Lake

Deep in the Highlands, at the end of a series of narrow and winding roads is Eagles Lake, one Victoria's best places to swim. The municipal park features a unique outhouse and a sand beach.

FACTS

Surface Area	0.5 ha
Elevation	122 m
Land Status	Municipal Park

ACTIVITIES

Swimming	Good swimming.
Hiking	None.
Cycling	Access via Munns Rd.
Boating	No motorized boats. Easy access for carry-in boats.
Picnics	Main beach is suitable for picnics.
Pets	Must be on a leash at the main beach.

FACILITIES

Beach	Yes.
Washrooms	Outhouse.
Accessibility	Easy access to the main beach.

Eagles Lake through the trees. Photo by Adam Ungstad.

DIRECTIONS FROM VICTORIA

1. *Head north on Douglas St (Trans-Canada Hwy)*

2. *Take Exit 8 toward View Royal*

3. *Merge onto Helmcken Rd N*

4. *Turn left onto Burnside Rd W*

5. *Turn right onto Prospect Lake Rd*

6. *Turn left onto Munn Rd*

8. *Turn right onto Westridge Pl*

9. *Take the 1st left onto Woodridge Pl*

10. *Turn right onto Eagles Lake Rd*

Eagles Lake is a swimmer's paradise that feels like it was taken straight out of a story-book.

The lake is a small, hidden classic swimming hole where if you didn't know better you'd expect to find a swing made out of an old tire and rope hanging over the water. Unless you are lucky enough to have someone tell you where Eagles Lake is, you probably would never find it.

The main beach and almost half of the shoreline falls within a municipal park, and there are a handful of residences a good distance away from the shore on the eastern side.

One of the lake's unique features is a composting toilet that was built by volunteers of the Highlands Parks and Recreation Association and Eco-Sense. This luxury outhouse features walls made of clay, sand, and straw, a living roof, and a time capsule within its walls containing a report produced by a sustainability task force. A composting toilet converts human waste into high quality compost, and this structure was built to last for 500 years.

Aside from being the smallest lake suitable for swimming in this book, Eagles Lake is also unique among its peers as it is very young. While the other lakes in the Highlands were created by glaciers about 13 000 years ago, Eagles Lake was created in 1976 by the removal of spring-fed wetland.

Did you know?
Eagles Lake was not named after birds circling the sky above as one might expect. The lake was actually named after civil servant Frank Eagles, who served in the 1960s. Eagles do live in the Highlands area however, so you may just happen to see one while visiting Eagles Lake!

The composting toilet at Eagles Lake. Photo by Adam Ungstad.

Opposite: Canadian geese at Thetis Lake. Photo by Mike J Munroe.

View Royal

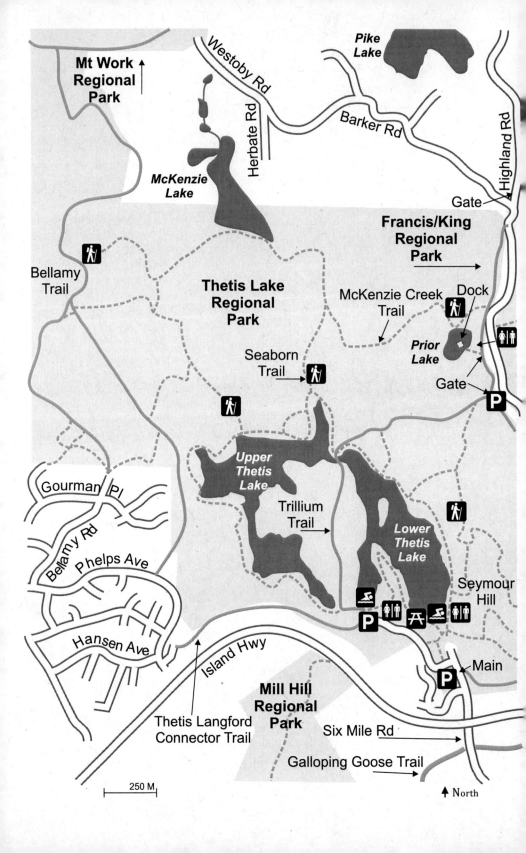

Thetis Lake

Thetis Lake is one of the larger, most used lakes in the area and will simply not disappoint. From the secluded coves along the shoreline to the cliffs and surrounding forest, Thetis Lake is a delight for visitors of all ages. This is also an ideal place to kayak, and a great destination for cyclists looking for a refreshing dip at the end of a bike ride.

FACTS

Surface Area 36 ha (Upper), 16 ha (Lower)

Max Depth 9 m

Elevation 60 m

Land Status Regional Park

ACTIVITIES

Swimming Great swimming.

Hiking Many hiking trails. A moderate to challenging trail circles the lake, with wilderness hiking trails branching off at the north end.

Cycling Access via the Galloping Goose Regional Trail and Six Mile Road.

Boating Boats with electric motors are permitted. Boat launch is at the second beach.

Fishing Rainbow trout (stocked in 2012).

Picnics Picnic tables at the main beach and plenty of viewpoints around the lake ideal for a picnic lunch.

Pets Must be under control and on trails. Dogs must be on a leash to pass through the main beach from June 1 – Sept 15.

FACILITIES

Beach Two sand beaches. See map for main beach and second beach. Many other secluded access points and rock outcrops throughout the lake.

Washrooms Available at the main beach and second beach.

Accessibility The lakeside trail to the west of the main beach is wheelchair accessible up to the second beach, and most trails around the lake are wide and well groomed.

DIRECTIONS FROM VICTORIA

1. Head north on Douglas St (Trans-Canada Hwy)

2. Take Exit 10 toward View Royal/Colwood

3. Slight right onto Old Island Hwy

4. Turn right onto Six Mile Rd

Thetis Lake exemplifies the best of Victoria's lakes for lake enthusiasts of all types. The lake with a unique shape offers it all: swimming, sunbathing, hiking, and access for non-motorized boats. The trails around the lake's beaches, cliffs, secluded coves, and surrounding forests offer an opportunity to connect with nature in its finest form.

A short walk from the main parking lot off Six Mile Road is the sandy Main Beach, which bustles in the summer with lake goers of all ages. There are washroom and changing facilities, picnic tables, a water fountain, and often food vendors. There is a small fee for parking during the summer, but the lot is rarely patrolled in the winter.

Often overlooked by those who stop at the main beach, the second parking lot on the southwest side of Lower Thetis has a smaller, shadier beach that is ideal for launching small boats or letting dogs get into the water. The trails around the shoreline of Thetis are also popular with dog walkers year round.

From an ecological perspective, Thetis Lake is surrounded by mid-growth hemlock, cedar, arbutus, and Douglas fir trees, offering a chance to see the variety of the flora southern Vancouver Island is best known for. In the springtime watch for wildflowers in the hills nearby, including shooting star, white fawn lily, and spring gold.

In the summer time dragonflies, damselflies, butterflies, moths, and caterpillars buzz, flutter, and crawl about. Thetis Lake is also home to many insects that go unseen -- either too small to be seen with the naked eye, or living under the water's surface. Watch the tree trunks for evidence of woodpeckers hunting for grubs and boring insects, as well as sap suckers in search of nectar from the trees. Moths and other insects are attracted to the sap, and in so doing become additional food for their avian predators.

At dusk watch for the bats that live in the hills nearby. They can be quite a sight as they socialize, swirl, and congregate around the lake. Deer, river otter, and even the occasional cougar also call Thetis Lake Park home.

Credit for the thriving ecosystem surrounding the lake is given in no small part to the Thetis Park Nature Sanctuary Association. The association was formed in 1957 with a mission to "protect, preserve and perpetuate the native flora and fauna of Thetis Lake Park," and is the first formal nature sanctuary in Canada.

HIKING

There is a series of trails one can take around Thetis Lake, making it perfect for hikers and walkers of various levels. A large gravel path circles the lake in two loops – one around the lower half and the second around the upper half. The lakeside trail offers a variety of views and access points. Perhaps the best-loved feature of Thetis Lake is its secluded coves, offering many quiet spots to spend an afternoon for anyone willing to explore.

Although the trail around the lake is considered moderate in difficulty, most able-bodied hikers will not have a problem circling it. Starting from the main beach, the trail on the west side (to the left) is an easier walk with less hills, while the east trail offers panoramic views of the lake from the cliff at the top of a hill. Recent improvements by the Capital Regional District have made the trail more accessible for everyone while helping to ensure the integrity of the surrounding ecosystem.

The exposed rock you will see from the trail is left over from an earlier ice age. In wetter parts of the trail rocks are covered with delicate, brilliant green mosses that offer homes for a variety of wildflowers.

The trail around the upper half of the lake is a bit rockier and undulating but still relatively flat. There are a handful of benches to be found that offer a chance to rest and enjoy the beautiful surroundings. Watch for salal berries and sword ferns in the undergrowth around the trails.

If the lakeside trail isn't enough, explore the network of single track trails at the north end of the park to nearby McKenzie Lake or Stewart Mountain.

Thetis Lake is a great place to be in the morning when mist surrounds its secluded coves.
Photo by Eric Anderson.

MCKENZIE LAKE & BELLAMY TRAILS

For those that enjoy a good, brisk hike through wilderness trails explore the rocky and sometimes narrow single track trail to McKenzie Lake, starting from the McKenzie Creek trail at the north end of Thetis Lake. Alternatively you may want to start at the Highland Rd entrance.

Be aware that McKenzie Lake is not a great place to swim however, as trees and shrubs surround the south shore of the lake (which is in the park land), and private homes take up the rest of the shoreline. The eastern half of the trail is an interesting hike however, leading through wetlands and across plank bridges and log rounds. Budget 2.5 hours for a round trip to McKenzie Lake and back if you're starting from the Main Beach at Thetis Lake.

For those looking for even more of a challenge, make the trek up the little known Bellamy trail to the Stewart Mountain and Scafe Hill. At over 830 hectares, this park has a lot to explore!

FRANCIS/KING PARK

Adjacent to Thetis Lake Park is Francis/King Park, a low elevation Douglas fir and grand fir forest with trees up to two meters thick, 75 meters high, and 500 years old.

The park offers an interpretive Nature House with staff, displays, and programming year-round, as well as the 750 metre wheelchair-accessible Elsie King Trail that leads through the forest on a cedar boardwalk.

On your walk watch for birds such as turkey vultures, hawks, woodpeckers, sapsuckers, hummingbirds, swallows, chickadees, and wrens. On the ground, look for snakes, frogs and ants! This is a great place to take the kids.

Did you know?
Although Thetis Lake was originally one lake, it was separated into two when a dike was installed to create access for a fire road. In later years a culvert was installed under the dike to link the two lakes again, thus allowing paddlers to explore both lakes. As such there is some debate over whether this is one lake or two – the BC Geological Survey states that the official name of the lake is "Thetis Lake," but that the feature type was changed from "lake" (singular) to "lakes" (plural) in 2003.

HISTORY

The woods near what is now known as Thetis Lake were long used by the Coast Salish to hunt deer, bear, and elk. They would also harvest clams from the harbour below, and would steam, mash, cook, and roast the native sprouts and berries found in the undergrowth for food.

Thetis Lake was named after a boat in the British navy – the HMS Thetis, a 36 gun sailing frigate that was sent to protect British rights to gold found in Haida Gwaiii (formerly the Queen Charlotte Islands) in 1852. In addition to the lake the nearby Thetis Island and Thetis Cove were also named after this ship.

Thetis Lake was one of the earliest sources of water for the City of Victoria. In the mid-1800s water from wells and creeks, such as Spring Ridge Commons, was taken into the city by horse and wagon and sold off of a cart for as much as 25 cents per bucket. In 1864 the Spring Ridge Water Company laid log pipes to transport water from the Elk Lake to downtown Victoria. Thetis Lake was connected to this system as a reserve supply in the 1870s. Water was then transported from Sooke Lake in the early 1900s.

Thetis Lake was not designated as a park until 1993 when the City of Victoria transferred the land to the Capital Regional District – this was done due to tax reasons (municipalities pay more taxes for parkland than they do for land that supplies water). The lake has been open to the public for recreation and swimming since 1932 and was a game reserve until 1961.

While Thetis Lake is quite a large park today, bits and pieces of the park have been traded in order to preserve larger pieces of land in the Victoria area. In 1960, 105 acres of land at the north end of Thetis Lake Park was given to BC Electric in exchange for 204 acres surrounding Durrance Lake – this trade was done to enable the placement of power lines that can be seen when driving up Munn Road through Francis / King Park. Likewise, the water levels in the lake were raised in 1979 to enable trout to spawn in Craigflower Creek at the cost of 360 drowned trees along the shoreline of the lake.

Did you know?
There is a private campground adjacent to the park property that offers easy tent camping (with showers!) in close proximity to the city. A great place to stay with the kids.

Prior Lake

A local clothing optional favourite. Prior Lake has a sand beach and a dock that are ideal for sunbathing or jumping into the refreshing water.

FACTS

Surface Area	2 ha
Max Depth	5 m
Elevation	40 m
Land Status	Regional Park

ACTIVITIES

Swimming	Good swimming, very warm water.
Hiking	No trails around the lake, but access to the McKenzie Creek trail is off of Highland Rd. Parts of the park are marked as under restoration – stay out of these areas as this is a dedicated nature sanctuary.
Cycling	Access via the Galloping Goose Regional Trail. Exit at Burnside Rd W, turn left on Watkiss Way, and follow Highland Rd to the lake. Cycling not permitted on trails in the park.
Boating	No motorized boats.
Fishing	Cutthroat trout and rainbow trout (stocked 2011).
Picnics	No picnic tables, but the dock and beach are available.
Pets	Dogs not permitted on the dock or at the main beach from June 1 – Sept 15. The beach and dock are a relatively small space without walking trails, so it is best to take dogs to a different beach if possible.

The beach and dock at Prior Lake buzz with activity in the summer months.
Photo by Adam Ungstad.

FACILITIES

Beach   Beach and dock.

Washrooms   Outhouse.

Accessibility   The short 1 km gravel trail descending to the beach is a bit steep at points and is generally not considered wheelchair accessible, but it has been done before.

DIRECTIONS FROM VICTORIA

1. *Head north on Douglas St (Trans-Canada Hwy)*

2. *Take Exit 10 toward View Royal/Colwood*

3. *Keep right at the fork, follow signs for Burnside Road W*

4. *Turn left onto Watkiss Way*

5. *Follow the bend onto Highland Rd*

6. *Once you've entered the park continue past the first gate (for Thetis Lake)*

7. *Park outside the second gate (for Prior Lake).*

Prior Lake is a tiny paradise that has been used by naturists for as long as anyone can remember. A naturist, not to be confused with a naturalist, is a person who seeks to enjoy nature in a completely natural state – that is, without clothing. The lake's natural beauty, small size, warm water, and ease of access make it one of the best places to swim and sunbathe in the area.

The philosophy of naturism includes being considerate and respectful of others, and on your first visit to Prior Lake you will find naturists to be friendly and very respectful of others, as well as the natural environment around them. Prior Lake generally has a more laid-back, mature feel to it than its noisier neighbour. If you are hesitating on your visit to Prior Lake because you are not sure what to expect, take the plunge. You will be glad you did!

There is a small beach and a dock that goes out into the lake. If you go on a hot summer afternoon you'll find plenty of sunbathers on the dock – but there's always room for more. The dock generally keeps all lake goers in close proximity, so expect some social activity while you are there. Bring an air mattress or a tube to float on if you'd prefer a little more space to yourself.

To really know Prior Lake you need to go there at dusk on a late summer's evening. Enjoy the silhouettes of the trees around you while you swim through the silky water and listen to the serenade of the pacific tree frogs who call the lake home.

HISTORY

There have been three docks at Prior Lake throughout the years. The first one was very small and known to sink below the waterline when it got crowded. The second, much larger dock was provided by the City of Victoria, but then subsequently removed when Thetis Lake Park was transferred to the Capital Regional District (CRD) in 1993. The naturists who had been enjoying the dock for decades mobilized to raise funds towards the construction of a new dock, which the CRD provided the remainder of financing for and constructed in 1994.

Prior Lake was originally known as 'Little Thetis Lake,' and acquired its current name in 1934 after Lieutenant-Colonel The Honorable Edward Gawlor Prior, a man whose history is deeply interwoven with the development of Victoria. Mr. Prior arrived to Vancouver Island in 1873 and was originally employed as a mining engineer. He later went on to lead an influential career in business and politics.

In 1878 Edward Prior owned a hardware store in a building that still stands at the corner of Government and Johnson Street in downtown Victoria – across Government Street from where the Mountain Equipment Co-op is currently located. The staff at his store would go on fishing trips out to Sooke Lake together. Mr. Prior later moved into politics, being elected to the provincial legislature in the late 1880s and 1890s, eventually serving as the Premier of British Columbia from 1902–1903. Long known as a hard worker, Mr. Prior died in 1920 while serving as Lieutenant Governor.

Did you know?
Prior Lake is a great alternative to Thetis Lake for cyclists looking for a good bike ride and a swim. Exit the Galloping Goose trail when it crosses Burnside Road West, turn left on to Watkiss Way, and keep following the road until you enter Thetis Lake Park. Watch for the second gate on your left, about 10 minutes after entering the park. The last bend on Watkiss Way as it turns into Highland Road is a fairly steep incline, but remember that you'll get to ride down this hill on your way back after a refreshing swim!

Opposite: A sign at the entrance to Lookout Lake reveals the popularity of the lake. Photo by Adam Ungstad.

NO ROPE SWINGS PERMITTED

LOOKOUT LAKE PARK

1. No supervision is provided by the City of Colwood.

2. This trail is intended for pedestrians.

3. For maintenance issues, please call Colwood Public Works at 250-474-4133.

4. In case of an emergency, call 911.

Colwood

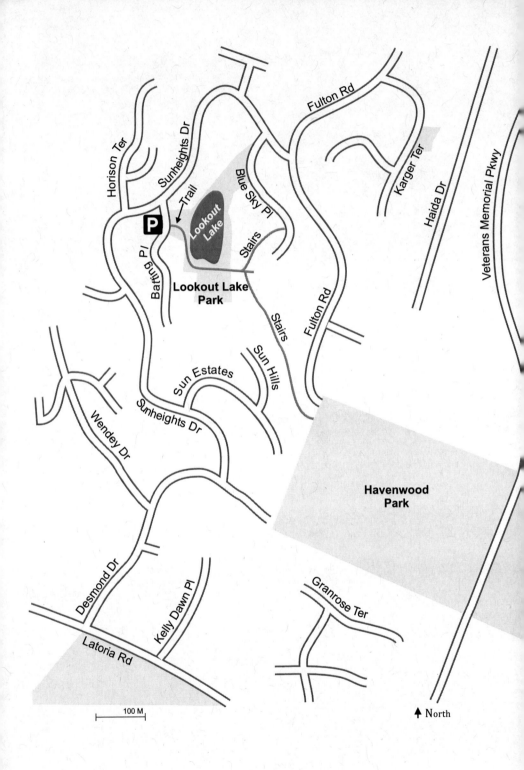

Lookout Lake

FACTS

Surface Area   0.5 ha

Max Depth   157 m

Land Status   Municipal Park

ACTIVITIES

Swimming   Good swimming, but expect to share the shoreline with fishers.

Hiking   No hiking trails, but plenty of steep stairs above and below the park that offer a good workout and unique views of the area.

Cycling   Access via the Galloping Goose Trail, Jacklin Rd, Sooke Rd, and Fulton Rd. Cycling on roads is required to reach Lookout Lake.

Boating   Suitable for carry-in boats, but the small size of the lake may make it not worth the effort to launch a boat.

Fishing   Rainbow trout (stocked in 2012) and smallmouth bass.

Picnics   No picnic tables, but the main beach is a sunny, open area ideal for picnic blankets.

FACILITIES

Beach   Features a wide sand beach that is a bit rocky at some points. Great for sun tanning.

Washrooms   None.

Accessibility   Easy access to the main beach via a small and level trail. The short trail may be a bit steep for a wheelchair however.

Lookout Lake is a popular place for swimmers and fishers alike. Photo by Adam Ungstad.

Perched up high on Triangle Mountain is Lookout Lake, a local favourite for swimming, sun tanning, and shoreline fishing. The popularity of this municipal park is best evidenced by the sign at the main entrance which reads, "No Rope Swings Permitted."

A footpath on the north-west side of the lake leads to an alternative access point to the water, so take some time to explore if you'd like to be a bit removed from the commotion at the main beach. This footpath is also accessible from Blue Sky Place.

Stairs at the end of the main beach lead up to the hill's summit which is crowned with private homes but offers an occasional glimpse of the surrounding vista including Victoria and the Olympic mountains to the south. On the other hand, following the set of stairs down will take you to Havenwood Park.

While the lake is best known for its fishing opportunities, humans aren't the only ones that enjoy the abundant fish at this lake – watch for eagles as they swoop down to catch their next meal.

Opposite: A viewing platform at the end of Leigh Road leads up the west side of the lake to Goldstream Meadows Park via the Ed Nixon trail. Photo by Adam Ungstad.

BOARDWALK
SURFACE MAY
BE SLIPPERY
WHEN FROSTY
OR WET

Langford

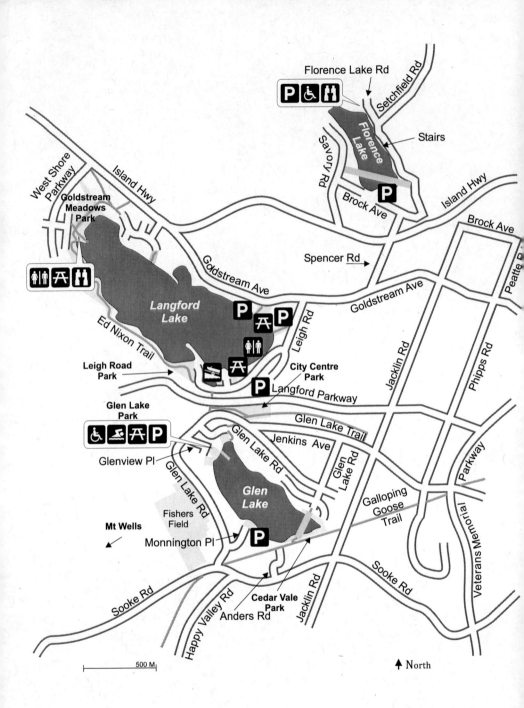

Florence Lake Rd

Setchfield Rd

Stairs

Florence Lake

Savory Rd

Island Hwy

Brock Ave

Brock Ave

West Shore Parkway

Island Hwy

Goldstream Meadows Park

Spencer Rd

Goldstream Ave

Goldstream Ave

Peatte Rd

Langford Lake

Ed Nixon Trail

Leigh Rd

Jacklin Rd

Phipps Rd

Leigh Road Park

City Centre Park

Langford Parkway

Glen Lake Park

Glen Lake Trail

Glenview Pl

Jenkins Ave

Glen Lake Rd

Glen Lake Rd

Glen Lake Rd

Galloping Goose Trail

Parkway

Mt Wells

Fishers Field

Glen Lake

Monnington Pl

Veterans Memorial

Sooke Rd

Cedar Vale Park

Jacklin Rd

Sooke Rd

Happy Valley Rd

Anders Rd

500 M

↑ North

Langford Lake

Located in the heart of a fast growing municipality, Langford Lake is a popular destination for fishing, boating, and swimming. Numerous access points provide opportunities for picnics, while walkers and dog owners will enjoy the Ed Nixon Trail leading from Leigh Rd to Goldstream Meadows Park at the north end.

LANGFORD

FACTS

Surface Area	61 ha
Max Depth	17 m
Elevation	67 m
Land Status	Municipal Park / Private Land

ACTIVITIES

Swimming	Good swimming.
Hiking	Ed Nixon Trail is an easy walk around the south, west, and north sides of the lake.
Cycling	Bicycles are permitted on the Ed Nixon Trail.
Boating	Boat trailer launch at Leigh Road.
Fishing	Rainbow trout (stocked 2012). Fishing platforms at Leigh Rd boat launch as well as the north end of the lake in Goldstream Meadows Park.
Picnics	Numerous parks suitable for a picnic. For a quiet spot choose Goldstream Meadows Park at the north end of the lake.
Pets	Dogs permitted provided they are under control.

FACILITIES

Beach   None.

Washrooms   Available at Leigh Road boat launch and Goldstream Meadows park.

Accessibility   The Ed Nixon Trail is wheelchair accessible.

DIRECTIONS FROM VICTORIA

1. *Head north on Douglas St (Trans-Canada Hwy)*

2. *Turn left onto Spencer Rd*

3. *Turn right onto Goldstream Ave*

4. *Turn left onto Leigh Rd*

5. *Follow Leigh Rd to the end*

At 61 hectares in size, Langford Lake is the largest lake in the area. It has many board-walks and access points that provide great swimming and fishing opportunities, and a boat launch on Leigh Road ensures access for kayaks, canoes, and other non-motorized boats.

The lake is a favourite for fishing, offering good sized rainbow trout, small-mouth bass, cutthroat, and perch. The lake is stocked with Cutthroat trout each year.

The main boat launch is at the end of Leigh Road, where a floating viewing platform provides recreation for hikers, swimmers, and picnickers year round. The viewing platform is also accessible on foot from Goldstream Avenue via the Leigh Road Trail.

The Ed Nixon Trail, named after the owner of the gravel pits at the north end of the lake, continues from the boat launch to Goldstream Meadows Park at the north end. Alternatively, heading south from the boat launch leads to the City Centre Park and continues to the Glen Lake Trail.

The swimming platform at the end of Leigh Road is popular during the summer months.
Photo by Adam Ungstad.

HISTORY

Langford Lake was named after Captain Edward Langford, who immigrated to Vancouver Island after retiring from the British Navy in 1834. While he was tasked with managing a 200 acre farm for a subsidiary of the Hudson's Bay Company in the Colwood area, Langford was known for keeping an open house for potential suitors for his five daughters.

While Captain Langford returned to England in 1861, his enterprising spirit persisted in the area, with wilderness lodges and cabins built for hunters and fishers around the lake in the years following.

The construction of the Esquimalt and Nanaimo (E&N) railway in the 1880s drove more visitors to the area, although passengers continuing past would never know about Langford Lake as it was hidden from view behind dense forest.

By the 1930s, summer cottages had outnumbered the hunting lodges around the lake. Residents of the area were known for hosting fantastic summer picnics, along with annual regattas that featured distance swimming, row boat races, and a chance to play summer games while frolicking in the west coast heat.

Today most of the original lodges and cabins have been replaced by modern homes, but a few remaining cottages can be recognized by their distinctive chimneys.

The boardwalk at Glen Lake provides a nice place to sit and relax
... or to fish! Photo by the City of Langford.

An accessible fishing pier at Glen Lake provides views and fishing
opportunities year around. Photo by the City of Langford.

Glen Lake

An urban haven for canoes and kayaks, with an accessible fishing pier, picnic tables and sand beach. Direct access off the Galloping Goose Regional Trail.

FACTS

Surface Area	16.8 ha
Max Depth	14 m
Elevation	67 m
Land Status	Municipal Park / Private Land

ACTIVITIES

Swimming	Good swimming. Watch for turtles.
Hiking	None.
Cycling	Direct access off from the Galloping Goose Regional Trail.
Boating	Carry-in boat launch at Glen Lake Park.
Fishing	Rainbow trout (stocked in 2012), Cutthroat trout and Smallmouth bass. A fishing pier provides easy access to the lake.
Picnics	Picnic tables at Glen Lake Park.
Pets	Must be under control and on trails.

FACILITIES

Beach	Sand beach at Glen Lake Park.
Washrooms	Available at Glen Lake Park.
Accessibility	Glen Lake Park offers easy access to picnic tables, a sand beach and fishing pier.

DIRECTIONS FROM VICTORIA

1. *Head north on Douglas St (Trans-Canada Hwy)*

2. *Turn left onto Spencer Rd*

3. *Turn left to stay on Spencer Rd*

4. *Turn left onto Goldstream Ave*

5. *Turn right onto Jacklin Rd*

6. *Turn right onto Jenkins Ave*

7. *Turn right onto Glen Lake Rd*

8. *Take the 2nd left onto Glenview Pl*

9. *Turn right onto Shore View Dr*

South of Langford Lake is a haven for paddlers of all sorts. Canoes and small boats can be launched on the south end of the lake, at Glen Cove Park. Glen Clove Park also features a small boardwalk and is a great place to watch lily pads grow from spring into the fall.

The northern bank has picnic tables under Douglas fir and willow trees, as well as an accessible viewpoint that juts out a ways from the shore, doubling as fishing platform. An aeration system in the lake improves the water quality and therefore the standard of fishing. Expect to find rainbow trout, cutthroat trout, and small-mouth bass.

The Cy Jenkins trail runs along the southern edge of the lake and connects with the Galloping Goose Regional Trail and the commercial centre of Happy Valley.

HISTORY

Glen Lake was largely unknown to anyone but locals until the opening of the Galloping Goose Railway encouraged land owners to subdivide their properties for summer cottages. The railroad has since been removed and turned into a multi-use trail that is part of a network that stretches from the Swartz Bay ferry terminal to Sooke.

For more about the history of Glen, Langford and Florence lakes be sure to find a copy of *Old Langford* by Maureen Duffus.

Florence Lake

Langford's most hidden lake, Florence Lake provides an opportunity to walk above wetlands, a great place to swim, and an accessible viewing platform for calming views and fishing opportunities.

FACTS

Surface Area	9 ha
Max Depth	5.5 m
Elevation	81 m
Land Status	Municipal Park / Private Land

ACTIVITIES

Swimming	Good swimming. Access via stairs from Florence Lake Rd. Watch for turtles.
Hiking	The Strachan Trail provides an easy, accessible walk around the lake.
Cycling	Direct access off from the Galloping Goose Regional Trail.
Boating	Carry-in boats can be launched from the north shore.
Fishing	Rainbow trout. Viewing platform at the north end of the lake offers fishing opportunities.
Picnics	No picnic tables but benches can be found on the north and south ends of the lake. Must be under control and on trails.
Pets	Must be under control and on trails.

FACILITIES

Beach	No beach, but stairs from Florence Lake Rd provide access.
Washrooms	None.
Accessibility	The Strachan Trail is mostly accessible, with the exception of a steep hill from Savory Road. The viewing platform at the north end offers easy access and close parking.

A boardwalk stretches over wetland on the south side of Florence Lake.
Photo by Adam Ungstad.

DIRECTIONS FROM VICTORIA

1. *Head north on Douglas St (Trans-Canada Hwy)*

2. *Turn right onto Spencer Rd*

3. *Turn right onto Brock Ave*

4. *Turn left onto Florence Lake Rd*

Hidden behind a busy intersection of the TransCanada Highway, Florence Lake is virtually unknown to both visitors and locals alike. The lake offers views and fishing year around, with swimming opportunities in the summer and a colourful display of leaves in the fall. Skirt Mountain can be seen to the northwest.

The Strachan trail provides easy access and a pleasant walk around the east and southern sides of the lake, with boardwalks and viewing points throughout. The trail also provides numerous places to fish from the shore, and there is a boat launch on the north shore for carry-in boats.

Be sure not to miss the boardwalk between Savory and Brock roads on the south end of the lake. Raised well above ground level, this boardwalk provides a unique opportunity to examine some of the surrounding trees and hanging moss from a different perspective. Keep an eye out for song birds and small critters below while you admire the panoramic view of the lake.

HISTORY

There is some debate about who Florence Lake was named for. While the Geographic Survey of BC's registry of Geographic Names states that the lake was named after Florence Isabella Langford, Captain Langford's fifth daughter, other local historians believe it was named after other early settlers in the area, Henry and Florence Dumbleton.

Savory Road takes its name from the Savory family, who grew and sold vegetables in the Fernwood area of Victoria. In 1910 their business was growing so they bought 200 acres of land in Langford to expand their operations. The first Langford Gun Club was established on their property a few years later.

Did you know?

Unconfirmed local lore tells the story of a piano at the bottom of Florence Lake. Houses were built on the west side of the lake before there were roads to them, meaning the only way to transport large things like furniture was by boat. Apparently one owner tried to bring a piano to their home, and lost the piano in the lake when the boat capsized. If this is a true story the piano is likely still there.

Metchosin

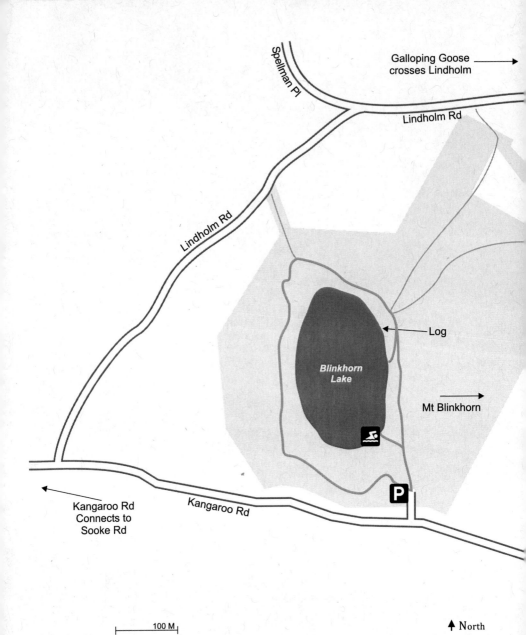

Galloping Goose
crosses Lindholm

Spellman Pl

Lindholm Rd

Lindholm Rd

Log

Blinkhorn
Lake

Mt Blinkhorn

P

Kangaroo Rd
Connects to
Sooke Rd

Kangaroo Rd

100 M

↑ North

Blinkhorn Lake

Metchosin's hidden beauty. Blinkhorn Lake is an ideal place to take the dogs for a walk and avoid the crowds at larger lakes nearby.

FACTS

Surface Area	2 ha
Max Depth	6 m
Elevation	123 m
Land Status	Municipal Park

ACTIVITIES

Swimming	Good swimming. Watch for turtles.
Hiking	An easy trail circles the lake with single track trails branching off the north end to Lindholm Rd.
Cycling	Access via the Galloping Goose and Lindholm Rd.
Boating	No motorized boats.
Fishing	Rainbow trout (stocked in 2010).
Pets	Must be under control and on trails.

FACILITIES

Beach	A small sand beach provides access to the water on the south (shady) side.
Washrooms	None.
Accessibility	Trail around the lake is very even and well-groomed. Recent improvements have added gravel to muddy sections.

Trees surround most of the shoreline at Blinkhorn Lake. Photo by Adam Ungstad.

DIRECTIONS FROM VICTORIA

1. *Head north on Douglas St (Trans-Canada Hwy)*

2. *Take Exit 14 toward Langford/Sooke/Highlands*

3. *Keep left at the fork, follow signs for McCallum Road W*

4. *Merge onto Millstream Rd S*

5. *Millstream Rd S turns into Veterans Memorial Pkwy*

6. *Turn right onto Sooke Rd*

7. *Turn left onto Kangaroo Rd*

Quietly shimmering away in the heart of Metchosin, Blinkhorn Nature Park is an ideal place to go for a walk to get away from it all. There is an easy 40 minute stroll through a peaceful forest of Douglas fir and western red cedar surrounding this small lake.

A small beach can be found on the south shore close to the Kangaroo Road parking lot, though it doesn't get much sun in the afternoon, so it's best to bring something to float on if you intend to swim or soak up sunshine. Chances are good that you'll have the lake to yourself if you do venture into the water.

An interesting feature of this lake is a fallen log at the northeast corner. While walking along the main trail you'll notice a puzzling clearing to the left that seems to serve no purpose as there is no direct access to the lake. Walk along the large log through the bushes however, and you'll find a cozy place from which you can enjoy the lake – an ideal place for a romantic picnic.

Another highlight to watch for is a small rise between the trail and the lake on the south side, where you'll find the remains of a cabin and a huge deciduous tree. Directly to the east of the lake is the 259 metre high Mount Blinkhorn, which is not part of the park.

HISTORY

Blinkhorn Lake gets its name from an energetic, enterprising and free-spirited fellow named Thomas Blinkhorn. Blinkhorn was the first truly independent settler to live in this vicinity – that is, he was the first settler in the area who was not a direct employee of the Hudson's Bay Company.

While most of the early pioneers arrived on Vancouver Island directly from England, Thomas Blinkhorn and his family had been raising stock in Australia for 12 years before moving to Vancouver Island in 1849.

The Blinkhorns ran the Bilston Farm in the area that we now call Witty's Lagoon, and for many years their farm was the only settlement between Sooke and Fort Victoria. Thomas Blinkhorn's wife Anne and his niece Martha tended the farm, thereby enabling Mr. Blinkhorn to pursue a political life. Martha kept a diary from 1853-1856 which is the only known diary written by a woman on Vancouver Island prior to the goldrush.

At the time there were First Nations people living on the beach below the farm. The Blinkhorns would hire their canoes as guides to Fort Victoria. In 1867 the Blinkhorns sold their farm to John Witty, a British Loyalist who had left the San Juan Islands for political reasons.

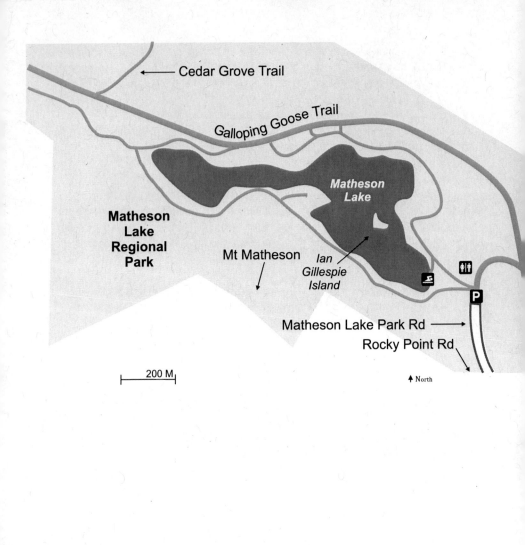

← Cedar Grove Trail

Galloping Goose Trail

Matheson
Lake

**Matheson
Lake
Regional
Park**

Mt Matheson

*Ian
Gillespie
Island*

Matheson Lake Park Rd →

Rocky Point Rd

200 M

↑ North

Matheson Lake

At over 160 hectares, Matheson Lake Regional Park offers just about anything a person could want from a lake. A sand beach, hiking trails, and direct access from the Galloping Goose Regional Trail make Matheson a favourite for families and cyclists.

FACTS

Surface Area	25 ha
Max Depth	5 m
Elevation	21 m
Land Status	Regional Park

ACTIVITIES

Swimming Good swimming. Watch for turtles.

Hiking Trail circling the lake provides a good workout. The north east side is flat and easy, while the south west side is moderate to challenging.

Cycling Access from the Galloping Goose Regional Trail. Cycling not permitted in the park.

Boating Boats with electric motors permitted.

Fishing Stocked with Cutthroat and Rainbow trout.

Picnics Bring a blanket for the beach.

Pets Must be under control and on trails. Must be on a leash at the main beach from June 1 to Sept 15.

FACILITIES

Beach Large sandy beach close to the parking lot.

Washrooms Available close to the main beach.

Accessibility The short trail to the beach may not be wheelchair accessible. The near by Galloping Goose Regional Trail offers a wheelchair accessible stroll, but does not provide lake views.

Swimmers on Ian Gillespie Island at Matheson Lake. Photo by Adam Ungstad.

DIRECTIONS FROM VICTORIA

1. *Head north on Douglas St (Trans-Canada Hwy)*

2. *Take Exit 10 toward View Royal/Colwood*

3. *Slight right onto Island Hwy S*

4. *Continue onto Old Island Hwy S*

5. *Continue onto Sooke Rd S*

6. *Turn left onto Metchosin Rd*

7. *Turn right onto Happy Valley Rd*

8. *Take the 1st left onto Rocky Point Rd*

9. *Turn right onto Matheson Lake Park Rd*

Referred to as a "precious jewel" in a 1979 edition of the Victoria Times, Matheson Lake is a wonderful place with a sand beach, surrounding mid-growth forest, and plenty of trails to explore nearby. It will take several visits to truly know the nature of this magical place.

If you prefer being in the water rather than on the trails, swim from the main beach out to Ian Gillespie Island. This small island offers plenty of space to lie down and soak up the sun after a good swim. While you are there be sure to say a friendly hello to the colony of peaceful ants that calls the island home.

Leading through Douglas fir, arbutus, and western red cedar woods, the full lakeside trail takes about 2 -3 hours. It connects with the Galloping Goose Regional Trail and crosses Wildwood Creek before taking an incline up Mount Matheson on the south side. Watch for yellow skunk cabbage at the west end of the lake as well as chikadees, woodpeckers, and Steller's jay in the branches around you.

If you decide to hike the full trail, keep in mind that maps can be deceiving and that the south side of the lake requires a bit of endurance. If you venture to the south side be sure to wear better shoes than flip flops! The views of the lake make this effort worthwhile.

Matheson Lake is a local favourite for fishing, either from the shore, a boat, or a float tube. The lake is stocked with cutthroat and rainbow trout, and the fishing is best in April and May. If you don't mind carrying your boat about 300 meters from the car park it's possible to launch small boats from the main beach area. Boats with electric motors are permitted.

HISTORY

Matheson Lake and its neighbour, the 700 foot Mount Matheson, were named after Sir James Matheson, a prominent business man in Hong Kong in the early 1800s. It is not clear whether James Matheson ever visited the area.

The lake was originally referred to as 'Big Lake' in an early Victoria Directory, and was also known as Ash's Lake after Dr. John Ash who owned land in the area.

Before the Galloping Goose Railway was converted to a trail, the residents of Sooke would pack a lunch and walk along the rail line to Matheson Lake, making it an all-day outing. Many of them would return home at the end of the day with plenty of fish.

Did you know?
Aboriginal lore recounted by Chief Ed Underwood of the East Saanich First Nations band states that Matheson Lake is guarded by all-powerful giants called Sheyeyas. Superior in intelligence and larger than sasquatches, Sheyeyas are invisible and can take on any shape they wish. It is believed that the Sheyeyas took the shapes of swans to guard the lake in the past.

A glimpse of Matheson Lake through the trees on the lakeshore trail.
Photo by Adam Ungstad.

Quarantine Lake

North of Becher Bay and south east of Mount Matheson is the small, little-known Quarantine Lake. While the lake is quite close to Matheson Lake as the crow flies, it is relatively unknown because it falls within the Beecher Bay Indian Reserve, and there is no access to the public.

Yet one can't help but wonder where this lake got its name from. Quarantine Lake was the site where individuals entering Canada with communicable diseases in the late 1800s were quarantined. Throughout the 1880s and 1890s the quarantine station moved between different sites in the area, starting at Albert Head before moving to Quarantine Lake, and then on to William Head in 1893.

Following: A snake slithers through the still waters at Peden Lake. Photo by Tracy Clifford.

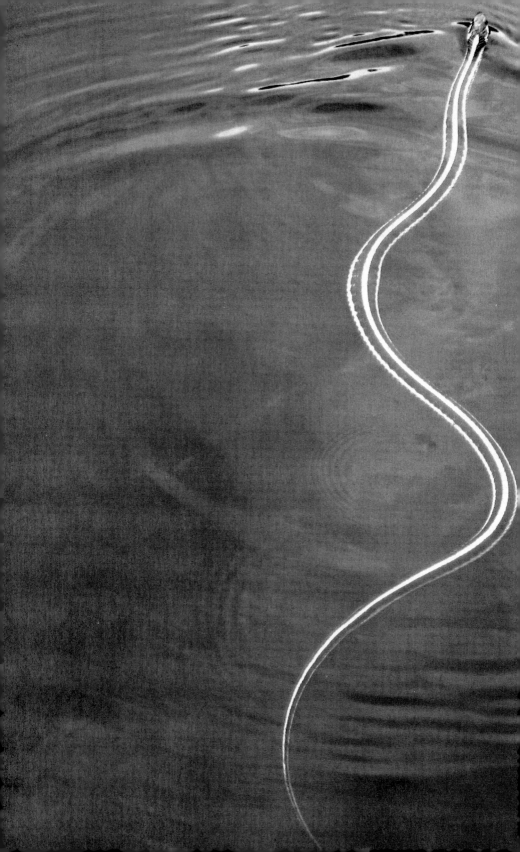

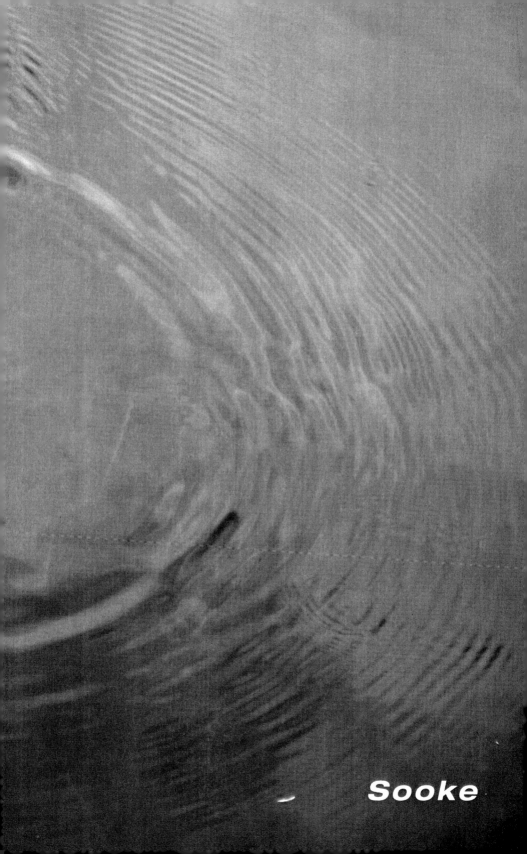

Sooke

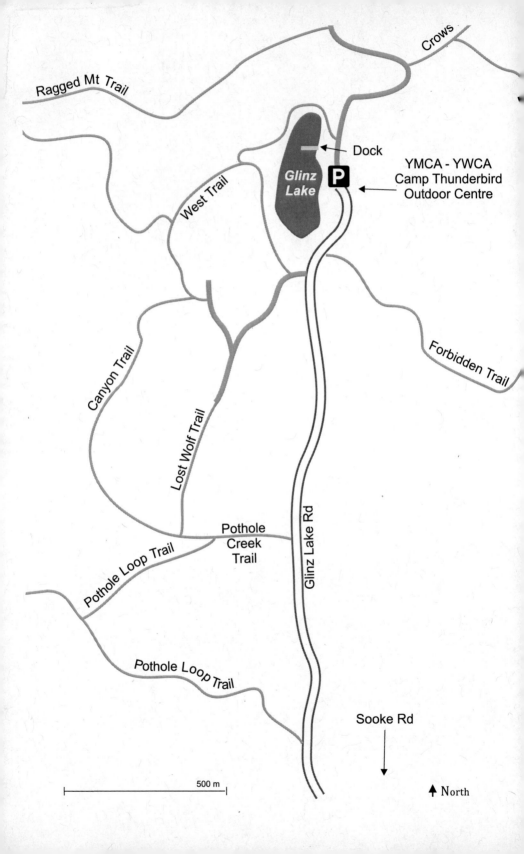

Glinz Lake

Glinz Lake is full of life and offers fantastic opportunities for learning about the nature of the area. In addition to offering summer programs for youth, the YMCA-YWCA owned Camp Thunderbird facility may be rented to host large groups.

FACTS

Surface Area	3.3 ha
Max Depth	10 m
Elevation	256 m
Land Status	Private Land

ACTIVITIES

Swimming	Good swimming.
Hiking	A large network of hiking trails around the lake.
Cycling	Access via the Galloping Goose and Glinz Lake Rd. Exit the Galloping Goose on Manzer Rd and cross Sooke Rd.
Boating	Carry-in boats only.
Fishing	Great fishing from the dock. Watch for rainbow trout jumping the surface in the fall.
Picnics	Numerous places suitable for picnics.
Pets	Must be under control and on trails.

A floating slide at Glinz Lake. Photo by Adam Ungstad.

FACILITIES

Rental Facilities Camp Thunderbird, run by the YMCA-YWCA, can be rented to accommodate groups of 20-250 people when summer camps are not in session

Beach The lake features a sand beach, dock, and an aquatic playground.

Washrooms Not available to public visitors.

Accessibility An easy trail with interpretive signs circles the lake. There are some wooden bridges and walkways so not all areas are wheelchair accessible.

A dock at Glinz Lake is perfect for fishing or swimming. Photo by Adam Ungstad.

DIRECTIONS FROM VICTORIA

1. *Head north on Douglas St (Trans-Canada Hwy)*

2. *Take Exit 14 toward Langford/Sooke/Highlands*

3. *Keep left at the fork, follow signs for McCallum Road W*

4. *Merge onto Millstream Rd S*

5. *Millstream Rd S turns into Veterans Memorial Pkwy*

6. *Turn right onto Sooke Rd*

7. *Turn right onto Glinz Lake Rd*

Moss growing on the roof of one of the Camp Thunderbird buildings.
Photo by Adam Ungstad.

Glinz Lake is found on the 1200 acre property of Camp Thunderbird, the unique outdoor branch of the YMCA-YWCA of Greater Victoria.

With facilities including a modern dining hall and a collection of cabins, Camp Thunderbird offers programming for youth in grades one through twelve with activities including swimming, canoeing, archery, orienteering, hiking, and teambuilding. Music and campfires follow in the evenings.

Facility rentals are also available to host groups of 20 to 250 people with an indoor gathering space, kitchen, cabins, and access to a beautiful lake and the network of trails leading through the surrounding forest.

Stocked with rainbow trout in mid1980s, Glinz Lake still offers excellent fishing. A dock in the middle of the lake is an ideal place to spend an afternoon gazing at dragonflies while catching your next meal.

Glinz Lake is also one of the best lakes on southern Vancouver Island to learn about the nature of the surrounding flora and fauna. An interpretive trail with hand-built bridges circles the lake, featuring signs that explain the surrounding forest and the creatures that live in it. Here you'll learn about the differences between trees like sitka spruce, red alder, western hemlock, grand fir and Douglas fir, just to name a few.

Along the trail you'll also learn about carnivorous beetles and slugs that decompose dead plants. Keep an eye and an ear out for song sparrows, lorquin's admirals and Steller's jay. And if you are there at just the right time you might even see a great horned owl!

HISTORY

Brothers Leonard and Arnold Glinz arrived to Vancouver Island from Switzerland in the early 1900s, and while exploring the wilderness of the Sooke area found the lake that now carries their family name. They decided the lake was an ideal place for a hunting cabin, but as there was no road to the lake they built their own, enabling them to bring hunting supplies three miles uphill.

The Glinz family kept the hunting cabin as a holiday and hunting retreat until the 1930s, and then decided to make it available as a children's camp.

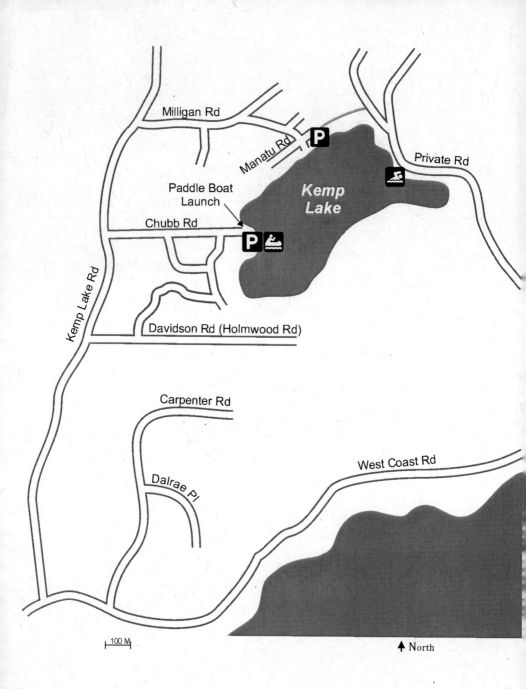

Kemp Lake

Found just past the municipality of Sooke, Kemp Lake is ideal for canoes and kayaks. Bring a picnic lunch to watch dragonflies circle water lilies. Aside from being a beautiful place to visit, the lake serves as a water source for the community living nearby.

FACTS

Surface Area	25 ha
Max Depth	11 m
Elevation	33 m
Land Status	Private Land / Municipal Access Points

ACTIVITIES

Swimming	Good swimming. Watch for turtles.
Hiking	A network of trails exists on the east side of the lake (Broom Hill). These trails are on private land.
Boating	Carry-in boat launch at Chubb Rd. Power boats not permitted.
Fishing	Cutthroat and rainbow trout (stocked in 2012).
Picnics	The best place for a picnic at Kemp Lake is on your canoe.
Pets	Must be under control and kept on trails.

FACILITIES

Beach	A sand beach can be found at the north-east corner of the lake. The beach is only accessible via canoe or kayak however, as the beach is not on public land.
Washrooms	None.
Accessibility	Chubb Rd provides an easy point to view the lake.

A beach on the north-east side of the lake offers a great place for paddlers to stop for a picnic.
Photo by Adam Ungstad.

DIRECTIONS FROM VICTORIA

1. *Head north on Douglas St (Trans-Canada Hwy)*

2. *Take Exit 14 toward Langford/Sooke/Highlands*

3. *Keep left at the fork, follow signs for McCallum Road W*

4. *Merge onto Millstream Rd S*

5. *Millstream Rd S turns into Veterans Memorial Pkwy*

6. *Turn right onto Sooke Rd*

7. *Follow Sooke Rd past the town of Sooke*

8. *Turn right onto Kemp Lake Rd*

9. *Turn right onto Chubb Rd*

If you are coming from the city the first thing you will notice getting out of your vehicle at Kemp Lake is the pristine, fresh ocean air in the Sooke area – the air at Kemp Lake alone will make your trip worthwhile!

Located just beyond the municipality of Sooke, this beautiful body of water is particularly well suited for non-motorized boats such as canoes, kayaks, and other rowboats. The boat launch and main access point is located off Chubb Road. Take a picnic lunch and watch for wildlife, dragonflies, and water lilies on the surface of the lake.

The east side of the lake, known as Broom Hill is currently private land, but local advocates are working to have the area become a park. And so they should – the network of trails in the area is an asset to the community.

A unique feature of Kemp Lake is that it is an active water source for approximately 750 people that live in the area. The Kemp Lake Waterworks District is managed by three elected trustees, with a new trustee being elected each year for a three year term.

Opposite: View from the north shore of Sheilds Lake. Photo by Adam Ungstad.

The Sea to Sea
Regional Park Reserve

The Sea to Sea Regional Park Reserve

Crabapple, Sheilds, Grass, and Peden lakes are found in the Sea to Sea Regional Park Reserve, an area of mid-growth wilderness sizeable enough to sustain entire ecosystems. Access to any of these lakes requires a 2-3 hour uphill hike on wilderness trails.

The landscape is dominated by mid-growth fir, cedar, hemlock trees with some groves Manzanita and arbutus, , and even pockets of Jack pine at the higher elevations. These forests provide habitat for many different species including bald eagles, black bears, cougars and sometimes even wolves. Be sure to stay on the trails and watch the ground below you for many types of colourful mushrooms, mosses and prolific ferns.

The park is within the T'Sou-ke Nation's traditional territory and has sustained thousands of years of First Nations culture. T'Sou-ke women gathered a range of forest products for medicinal, spiritual, household, and food use, and dug edible blue camas in owned and marked plots. Crabapple, Sheilds, and Grass Lakes were known as the "Smokehouse Lakes," where seasonal camps were set up to process fish and game for easier transport to the villages below. The T'Sou-ke First Nations remain active in the park development of the area.

While little physical evidence remains of aboriginal culture in the area, there are traces of enterprising pioneers of the early 1900s as well as forestry activity from as early as the1920s up to the1950s. Depending on the route you take and the lake you visit, you may discover old vehicles, pipelines, docks, and cabin sites.

The lakes in the Sea to Sea Regional Park Reserve are only accessible through a network of challenging and unmarked trails and an elevation gain of over 300 meters. There is no access for motorized vehicles or ATVs in the park, so count on a day-long hike or bike ride if you plan to visit them. Know your route, start early in the day, and bring a lunch, plenty of water, a GPS, and a friend.

A Park In Progress

The parcels of land within the Sea to Sea Regional Park Reserve make up about 3,874 hectares. The vision for the surrounding area, known as the Sea to Sea Green Blue Belt, is to create a corridor of 11,500 hectares of protected wilderness and parkland stretching across Vancouver Island from the Saanich Inlet to the Sooke Basin.

8,064 hectares of this land are currently held as provincial, regional, or municipal park land. The current holdings in the Sea to Sea Green Blue Belt include:
- Four CRD Regional Parks:
  - Ayum Creek
  - Sooke Potholes
  - Kapoor
  - Sooke Hills Wilderness Reserve
- The Sea to Sea Regional Park Reserve
- YMCA-YWCA Camp Thunderbird lands at Glinz Lake
- Sooke Mountain Provincial Park
- Goldstream Provincial Park
- Gowlland Tod Provincial Park

Local advocacy groups have been working towards the vision of a Sea to Sea Green Blue Belt for decades and recent years have yielded some exciting progress.

In August of 2010 the Capital Regional District (CRD), The Land Conservancy of BC (TLC) and the Province of British Columbia announced that 2,350 hectares of land in the Sooke Hills were purchased from Western Forest Products lands for a total cost of $18.8 million.

Aside from the Sea to Sea Regional Park Reserve, The Land Conservancy was also a partner in the acquisition of the nearby Sooke Potholes Campground and Ayum Creek Park, and has since launched the Wild Hills and Beaches campaign to work towards raising funds for further land acquisition in the Sea to Sea Green Blue Belt including parcels in Jordan River and Sandcut Beach. Donations can be made at www.conservancy.bc.ca.

The Capital Regional District has moved ahead with small developments including washrooms and a parking lot at the Harbourview Road entrance. In keeping with the nature of the area development of facilities at these lakes will be minimal, with plans for a composting toilet and backcountry campsite at Sheilds Lake.

Hiking the Smart Way

The Sea to Sea Regional Park Reserve is the home of bears, cougars, and wolves, so take precautions when you hike. There are no signs on any of the trails, so never hike alone as even a twisted ankle can leave you immobile. There is no reception for cell phones in most of the area, so be sure to tell a friend where you are going, what route you plan to take, and when you expect to be back.

This is a very large and unpatrolled area, so a first time visitor would be wise to make a smaller hike on their first visit to get to know the area a bit before venturing further. A day hike up to the ranger station at Mount Manuel Quimper would be a good first hike to get to know the area (and admire the view).

Carry plenty of water with you as you will be hiking all day and may need to share with your companions. Fruit, such as cherries or blueberries can help to hydrate you as well. To save space (and your back), consider buying a commercial water filter or sanitation tablets to enable you to drink lake water when you arrive. Bring enough food to ensure you have the energy for the return trip of your hike, but ensure that you leave no trace: pack your garbage out with you.

Depending on the time of year and the route you take you may need to cross a creek or small river, so good, sturdy footwear and an extra pair of socks will serve you well. Wear long sleeves and pants between April and May as tick activity can be unpleasant during these months. Taking a shower immediately when you return is recommended and will let you check your body for any ticks before they have buried themselves too deep.

Parts of the Harbourview Road trail within Sooke Mountain Provincial Park are washed out and inaccessible during the winter and spring. A detour was recently made around this part of the road however, so study the enclosed map of the area before you leave. Count on crossing small creeks regardless of the time of year or route you take in the Sea to Sea area – sturdy, waterproof gear is critical.

Last but not least, be aware of the risk of a wildfire. If you smoke, roll your own cigarettes and bring something to extinguish them in. Respect fire bans and CRD regulations at all times.

Crabapple Lake in early April. Photo by Dennis Kangasniemi & The Land Conservancy.

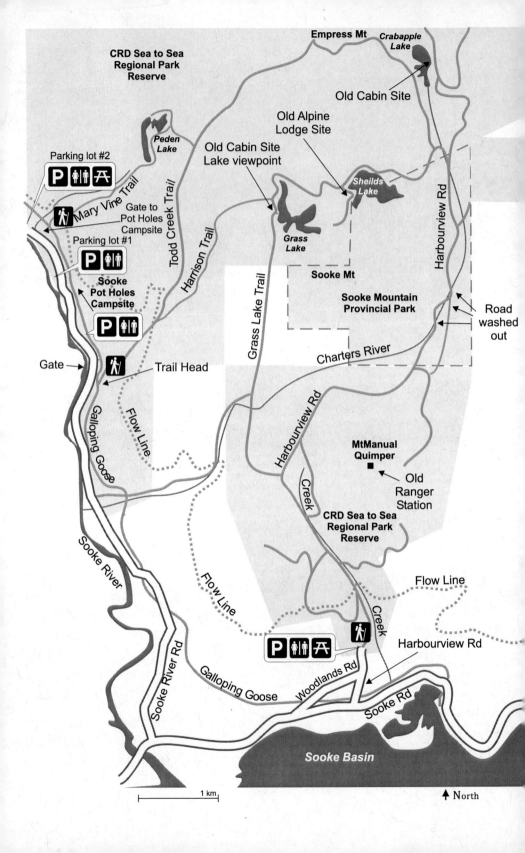

Crabapple Lake

A quiet beauty deep in the heart of the Sea to Sea Regional Park Reserve. Expect to find pink water lilies and solitude at this remote lake.

FACTS

Surface Area	6 ha
Max Depth	10 m
Elevation	427 m
Land Status	Regional Park Reserve

ACTIVITIES

Swimming — Good Swimming. Watch for salamanders, newts and pink water lilies.

Hiking — Moderate to challenging three hour hike (each way) via Harbourview Rd required to reach the lake. This is wilderness territory and you may encounter black bears or cougars. Never hike alone.

Cycling — The network of trails in the area are good for mountain biking. Harbourview Rd is steep at some points, and rocky at the north end.

Fishing — Rainbow and cutthroat trout (stocked 2009).

Picnics — No tables, but you'll definitely need to bring water and a lunch.

Pets — Must be on a leash at all times. This protects dogs and their owners from encounters with bears and cougars, as well as the forest undergrowth from being disturbed.

FACILITIES

Beach — Walk-in access to the lake.

Washrooms — Available at the Harbourview Rd trailhead, Sooke River Road, and Sooke Potholes Provincial Park. No facilities at the lake.

Accessibility — A lengthy, uphill hike on sometimes rocky trails is required to access Crabapple Lake.

DIRECTIONS FROM VICTORIA

1. *Head north on Douglas St (Trans-Canada Hwy)*

2. *Take Exit 14 towards Langford/Sooke/Highlands*

3. *Keep left at the fork, follow signs for McCallum Road W*

4. *Merge onto Millstream Rd S*

5. *Millstream Rd S turns into Veterans Memorial Pkwy*

6. *Turn right onto Sooke Rd*

7. *Turn right onto Harbourview Rd*

8. *Park at the trailhead, and follow Harbourview Rd Trail as shown on the map*

If you are looking for a lake to enjoy an afternoon of peace, quiet, and solitude with nature, Crabapple Lake is the one. Its remote location and high altitude mean that few people venture up to see it, and if they do they'll often head to the larger Sheilds Lake just to the west.

The best access to the lake is from the east side, and watch the treeline for a single Douglas fir tree with a diameter of over nine feet as you approach. In the summertime the shores are lined with pink lily pads, and there is a very old dock. A unique natural feature of Crabapple Lake is the seasonal presence of Canadian Geese, who have started using the lake only in recent years.

A cabin used to exist at Crabapple Lake in the mid 1900s but is gone now. The cabin had a stone fireplace and was built by early settler and forester Eric Bernard so he could share weekend retreats with his wife, Marjorie.

Like its neighbour Sheilds Lake, Crabapple Lake was used for skating in the winters of the mid 1900s.

Crabapple Lake is also the headwaters for the Charters River, which crosses the Harbourview Road trail at several points and eventually feeds into the Sooke River. Restoration and rehabilitation work done by volunteers and local governments has encouraged salmon spawning at the base of the river. You'll find rainbow and cutthroat trout at Crabapple Lake, so bring your fishing gear.

Sheilds Lake

At 16 hectares, Sheilds Lake is the largest of the lakes perched in the newly minted Sea to Sea Regional Park Reserve, and a stunning place to spend an afternoon.

FACTS

Surface Area	16 ha
Max Depth	16 m
Elevation	425 m
Land Status	Regional Park Reserve

ACTIVITIES

Swimming Good swimming. Watch for salamanders and newts.

Hiking Moderate to challenging three hour hike (each way) via Harbourview Rd or Harrison Trail required to reach the lake. This is wilderness territory and you may encounter black bears or cougars. Never hike alone.

Cycling The network of trails in the area are ideal for mountain biking. The Galloping Goose provides access to both Harbourview Road and the Harrison Trail. Harbourview Road access is recommended for Sheilds Lake as there is adequate parking and facilities at the trailhead.

Fishing Rainbow and cutthroat trout (stocked in 2009).

Picnics No tables, but you'll definitely need to bring water and a lunch.

Pets Must be on a leash at all times. This protects dogs and their owners from encounters with bears and cougars, as well as the forest undergrowth from being disturbed.

An island in the middle of Sheilds Lake.
Photo by Adam Ungstad.

FACILITIES

Beach	Many different access points to the lake.
Washrooms	Available at the Harbourview Rd trailhead, Sooke River Road, and Sooke Potholes Provincial Park. No facilities at the lake.
Accessibility	A lengthy, uphill hike on sometimes rocky paths is required to access Sheilds Lake.

DIRECTIONS FROM VICTORIA

1. *Head north on Douglas St (Trans-Canada Hwy)*

2. *Take Exit 14 toward Langford/Sooke/Highlands*

3. *Keep left at the fork, follow signs for McCallum Road W*

4. *Merge onto Millstream Rd S*

5. *Millstream Rd S turns into Veterans Memorial Pkwy*

6. *Turn right onto Sooke Rd*

7. *Turn right onto Harbourview Rd*

8. *Park at the trailhead, and follow Harbourview Rd Trail as shown on the map*

Nestled deep in the Sea to Sea Regional Park Reserve is Sheilds Lake, once known as the "Lake of the Seven Hills" after the mountains and peaks that surround it. You'll want to leave early for your hike to get to Sheilds Lake as time passes by pretty quickly once you are there.

This semi-alpine lake is a three hour uphill walk from the trail head, on a rocky old logging road that starts at the parking lot at the end of Harbourview Road. You can still see remnants of a paved road that enabled logging in the area in the 1940s and 1950s. Part of the road is badly washed out, so bring an extra pair of socks as you may need to wade through the small river. A detour around the washed out parts of the road was recently made however so be sure to study the map if you are hiking in the wet season.

The north side of the lake is the best, as it gets plenty of sun, and there is a rock outcrop at the northeast side perfect for a picnic or swimming. Parts of the trail around the lake have large puddles blocking the way, but look in the bushes nearby and you'll find detours around them. There is a rustic campsite with a picnic table at the southwest corner, but be aware that the trail does not circle the lake entirely.

You'll find rainbow and cutthroat trout at the lake, so bring your fishing gear. At one point in time a canoe was left at the lake for anyone to use, but it has since disappeared. At the south-west corner of the lake watch for the remains of an old lodge owned by the Alpine Club of Canada.

Because of its high altitude, the air at Sheilds Lake can be up to ten degrees cooler than at sea level, and sometimes sparkles with thin ice in January. As early as the 1940s Sooke residents would make the trek up to the lake to spend the day skating.

HISTORY

There is a persistent rumour that Sheilds Lake was intended to be known as "Sheila's Lake," but this is not true. Sheilds Lake was named after early settlers the Sheilds family, who owned a farm on the west side of the Sooke River in the 1890s.

One of the first settlers of the area was Claude L. Harrison, mayor, city prosecutor and also a member of the Alpine Club of Canada. Harrison leased 180 acres of the area to the Alpine Club of Canada and a two story lodge was built on the lake in 1928, proving to be a popular wilderness retreat in the 1930s. The lodge at Sheilds Lake has since burned down, but remains can be seen on the west side of the lake. Smaller cabins were also built at Sheilds Lake by Scouts Canada and the Boys Club of Victoria in the mid 1900s, but little physical evidence of either of these remains.

Eric Bernard, a man respected as running a well-known logging and pole-cutting operation in the area, paved a good deal of what we now know as Harbourview Road to support logging efforts in the 1940s and 1950s. The trail that continues at the end of Harbourview

Sheilds Lake in early April. Photo by Dennis Kangasniemi & The Land Conservancy.

Road was originally known as Mount Shepherd Road — pieces of the pavement can still be seen in the rockier sections of the trail. Bernard is also credited with bringing pink water lilies to Sheilds and Crabapple Lakes.

MOUNT EMPRESS

For a different perspective on Sheilds Lake, hike to the summit of the highest peak in the Capital Regional District, Empress Mountain, where spectacular vistas including a beautiful view of Sheilds Lake await. Using the map in the book, follow the Todd Creek trail from where it branches off of the Harrison Trail and continue past Peden Lake.

Grass Lake

Wetlands, marsh, lily pads, and a rocky outcrop great for a picnic and swimming deep in the Sea to Sea Regional Park Reserve.

FACTS

Surface Area	9 ha
Max Depth	7.6 m
Elevation	408 m
Land Status	Regional Park Reserve

ACTIVITIES

Swimming — Good swimming. Best access is on the rock outcrop on the south side of the lake.

Hiking — Moderate to challenging two to three hour hike up the Harrison Trail is required to reach the lake. This is wilderness territory and you may encounter black bears or cougars. Never hike alone.

Cycling — The Harrison Trail is accessible via the Galloping Goose and is ideal for mountain biking. There is no sign marking the start of the trail, but watch for a gate off of Sooke River Road that reads "No Motorized Vehicles."

Fishing — Cutthroat trout (stocked in 2009).

Picnics — No tables, but you'll definitely need to bring water and a lunch.

Pets — Must be on a leash at all times. This protects dogs and their owners from encounters with bears and cougars, as well as the forest undergrowth from being disturbed.

FACILITIES

Beach — Many different access points to the lake.

Washrooms — Available at the Harbourview Rd trailhead, Sooke River Road, and Sooke Potholes Provincial Park. No facilities at the lake.

Accessibility — A lengthy, uphill hike on a sometimes rocky trail is required to access Grass Lake.

Peaceful waters at Grass Lake. Photo by Tracy Clifford.

DIRECTIONS FROM VICTORIA

1. *Head north on Douglas St (Trans-Canada Hwy)*

2. *Take Exit 14 toward Langford/Sooke/Highlands*

3. *Keep left at the fork, follow signs for McCallum Road W*

4. *Merge onto Millstream Rd S*

5. *Millstream Rd S turns into Veterans Memorial Pkwy*

6. *Turn right onto Sooke Rd*

7. *Turn right onto Sooke River Rd*

8. *Park (off the pavement) at the gate to the Sooke Potholes Park*

9. *Follow the Harrison Trail as shown on map*

As one might expect, much of the shoreline around Grass Lake consists of wetlands and tall, marshy grass. Various maps show different shapes for this lake, indicating that water levels have changed its shape over time. There is a large outcrop on the south side of the lake that is the best place for a picnic and a swim after the lengthy uphill hike to get there.

If you are visiting during the summer months expect to find stunning water lilies of many shades floating on the surface of the lake. There used to be a cabin at the lake, and there is still an old wooden foot bridge that spans part of the trail on the west side.

THE HARRISON TRAIL

While Grass Lake is accessible via Harbourview Road and Sheilds Lake, experienced hikers who prefer wilderness trails would be best to take the Harrison Trail. This trail starts on Sooke River Road close to the gate to the Sooke Potholes Provincial Park, and takes about three hours to get to the lake. Watch for a gate with a sign that reads "No Motorized Vehicles," as that is the trailhead. Be sure to park outside of the park gates and that the tires of your vehicle do not touch the pavement, as your vehicle may be towed otherwise.

The Harrison Trail is not recommended for a first visit to the area and should always be hiked with a friend or two. There is a critical fork about 20-30 minutes into the hike after you pass the Galloping Goose Regional Trail – stay to the right to continue up to Grass Lake, as turning left will take you up the Todd Creek trail to Peden Lake and further on to the summit of Mount Empress. Be sure to start early in the day, take plenty of water, food, a GPS and a friend as there are no signs on the trail and no cellphone reception for most of the route.

Morning at Peden Lake. Photo by Tracy Clifford.

Peden Lake

FACTS

Surface Area	3 ha
Max Depth	316 m
Elevation	21 m
Land Status	Regional Park Reserve

ACTIVITIES

Swimming Good Swimming. Watch for salamanders and newts.

Hiking Moderate to challenging two hour hike (each way) via the Tod Creek Trail or Mary Vine Creek Trail required to reach the lake. This is wilderness territory and you may encounter black bears or cougars. Never hike alone.

Cycling Rugged wilderness trail requires a mountain bike. Access via the Galloping Goose.

Boating A canoe has been left at the lake for anyone to use. Paddles have a tendency to go missing however.

Fishing Cutthroat trout (stocked in 2009).

Picnics No tables, but you'll definitely need to bring water and a lunch.

Pets Must be on a leash at all times. This protects dogs and their owners from encounters with bears and cougars, as well as the forest undergrowth from being disturbed.

FACILITIES

Beach No sand beach, but walk-in access to the lake.

Washrooms None.

Accessibility A lengthy, uphill hike on sometimes rocky trails is required to access Peden Lake.

A fibreglass canoe at Peden Lake for anyone to explore, with the cabin in the background.
Photo by Tracy Clifford.

Peden Lake is known as a great swimming destination and an excellent day hike for campers staying at the Sooke Potholes Campground. There is a small one-room cabin that was recently built at the lake which has been respected by those who have visited to date. At the time of writing there was also a fibreglass canoe left for anyone wanting to explore. The lake actually consists of two separate bodies of water so be sure to take some time to explore the area. Peden Lake also makes for an excellent rest stop for those hiking up to the summit of Mount Empress.

There are two routes to get to Peden Lake, both of them starting from Sooke River Road, The first is the Todd Creek Trail, which branches off to the left of the Harrison trail shortly after it starts near the gate to the park. The second is the Mary Vine Creek Trail, a shorter and easier route that is currently under consideration for improvements in future phases of development for the Sea to Sea Regional Park Reserve.

HISTORY

Peden Lake was named after the Peden family, who owned a feed store on Wharf Street in Victoria for many years in the early 1900s and had two sons that grew up to be world famous athletes. William "Torchy" Peden was was born in Victoria in 1906, and acquired the nickname "Torchy" after his flaming red hair and ability to lead the pack of long distance cyclists. At the height of his successful career as a competitive cyclist in the 1930s, and in the midst of the great depression, Peden was given a gold-plated bicycle by the Canadian Cycle and Motor Company which he rode during special exhibitions. His brother, Douglas Peden, competed in the 1936 olympics and helped bring back a silver medal in basketball for Canada.

MARY VINE CREEK TRAIL

The Mary Vine Creek Trail is a moderately challenging wilderness trail that passes two water falls on its way up to Peden Lake. The trailhead is just to the north of the second parking lot in the Sooke Potholes Regional Park, and is relatively easy to follow despite a lack of signage.

Watch for a decision point about half a kilometre into the walk where you can continue straight or head east and up – remembering the lake's elevation, turn to the east and continue to follow the trail to the lake. With improvements to the trail under consideration this route is sure to become a local favourite.

Following: Picnic tables at the main beach of Spectacle Lake. Photo by Mark Gustafson.

Cowichan Valley Regional District

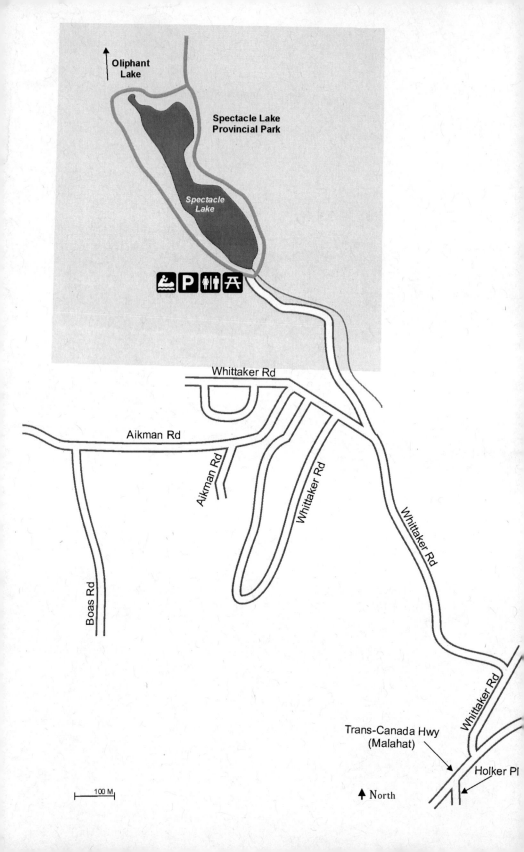

Spectacle Lake

A 65 hectare Provincial Park, Spectacle Lake is a great spot for swimming, canoeing, fishing or spending the day picnicking. It is also the only lake on southern Vancouver Island where you can fish for eastern brook trout.

FACTS

Surface Area	4 ha
Max Depth	7 m
Elevation	379 m
Land Status	Provincial Park

ACTIVITIES

Swimming	Good swimming.
Hiking	An easy 2 km trail leads around the lake, with further hiking opportunities to Oliphant Lake.
Cycling	None.
Boating	Boat launch for non-motorized boats.
Fishing	Eastern brook and cutthroat trout.
Picnics	Picnic tables at the main beach.
Pets	Must be under control and on trails.

FACILITIES

Beach	Small beach and plenty of access points to the water.
Washrooms	Available at the Main Beach.
Accessibility	Most parts of the trail are accessible. Some small wooden bridges.

An even and well groomed trail circles Spectacle Lake. Photo by Mark Gustafson.

DIRECTIONS FROM VICTORIA

1. *Head north on Douglas St (Trans-Canada Hwy)*

2. *The Trans Canada Hwy turns into the Malahat*

3. *Turn left onto Whittaker Rd*

Found about an hour northwest of Victoria on the Malahat Drive, Spectacle Lake was given its name because its shape which resembles a pair of glasses (spectacles). It's unique location ease of access and developed facilities make it a favourite for a stop between Victoria and Nanaimo.

There are picnic tables close to the parking lot, and an easy 2-kilometre, well-maintained hiking trail circles the lake through mature forest and wetlands, crossing wooden bridges over a few creeks feeding into the lake. Gaze through the clear water for a moment or two and you are sure to see crayfish scuttling along the lake bottom.

A boat launch is available for carry-in boats. Its high altitude (379 m) also makes Spectacle Lake a winter speciality: if the weather is cold enough the lake will freeze over, providing a reliable place to skate.

HISTORY

The area around Spectacle Lake has a rich history of logging. It was the site of a sawmill in the 1940s, which was located on the rocky outcrop close to the main beach. In the 1920s and 1930s the lake was dammed and used to boom logs. The area immediately around the lake was logged prior to 1960, and there are informal trails left from this time that connect Spectacle Lake to the much larger Oliphant Lake, the Malahat Ridge, and the Hatchet Jack Lookout Point.

USEFUL WEBSITES

Below are some websites you will find useful when visiting the lakes in this book.

ORGANIZATION

Freshwater Fisheries Society of BC	http://www.gofishbc.com/
Friends of Todd Creek Watershed	http://todcreek.rd123.ca/
Habitat Acquisition Trust	http://www.hat.bc.ca/
Prior Lake Naturist Preservation Committee	http://priorlake.wordpress.com/
Swan Lake Christmas Hill Nature Sanctuary	http://www.swanlake.bc.ca/
The Land Conservancy	http://blog.conservancy.bc.ca/
Thetis Park Nature Sanctuary Association	mmeagher@pfc.forestry.ca/
Vancouver Island Health Authority	http://viha.ca/
Victoria Natural History Society	http://vicnhs.bc.ca/

MUNICIPALITY

Capital Regional District (CRD)	http://www.crd.bc.ca/parks/
City of Colwood	http://www.colwood.ca/
City of Langford	http://www.cityoflangford.ca/
City of View Royal	http://www.viewroyal.ca/
Cowichan Valley Regional District	http://www.cvrd.bc.ca/
District of Highlands	http://highlands.bc.ca/
District of Metchosin	http://www.district.metchosin.bc.ca/
District of Saanich	http://www.saanich.ca/parkrec/parks/
District of Sooke	http://www.sooke.ca/

Freshwater Fishing Licence   http://www.fishing.gov.bc.ca/

Ministry of Environment   http://www.gov.bc.ca/env/

FURTHER READING

Below is a list of books and websites that were used to compile the information in this book. Use this list to learn more about what interests you.

BOOK	AUTHOR
Beacon Hill Park History 1842 - 2009 (website)	Ringuette, Janis
Beautiful Rocks	Highland Heritage Park Society
Craigflower Country: A History of View Royal	Maureen Duffus
Hiking Trails 1	Vancouver Island Trails Society
Hiking Vancouver Island	Cowan, Shannon
Metchosin Place Names	Page, Bess
Mountain Bike Vancouver Island	Cammiade, Daniel
Nature Walks Around Victoria	Landsdowne, Helen
Old Langford	Maureen Duffus
Recommendations for a District of Highlands Heritage Register	Highlands Heritage Task Force
Reflections on Prospect Lake	Prospect Lake Heritage Committee
The Naturalist's Guide to the Victoria Region	Victoria Natural History Society
The Victoria Naturalist (magazine)	Victoria Natural History Society
Victoria-Nanaimo Nature Walks	Bird in the Hand Enterprises

WEBSITES AND DATABASES

BC Geographical Names Search	http://archive.ilmb.gov.bc.ca/bcnames/
Beacon Hill Park History 1842 - 2009	http://www.beaconhillparkhistory.org/
Data BC	http://www.data.gov.bc.ca/
Fisheries Information Summary System	http://www.env.gov.bc.ca/fish/fiss/index.html
Hiking For Fat People	http://members.shaw.ca/hikingforfatpeople/
Vancouver Island Parks	http://www.vancouverislandparks.com/
Victoria Newspapers 1858 - 1932	http://web.uvic.ca/vv/newspaper/

ARCHIVES

BC Archives	http://www.bcarchives.bc.ca/
City of Victoria Archives	http://www.victoria.ca/
Greater Victoria Public Library	http://gvpl.ca/
Saanich Archives	http://www.saanich.ca/
Sooke Region Museum	http://www.sookeregionmuseum.com/